At Issue

Mexico's Drug War

Other Books in the At Issue Series:

At Issue

Mexico's Drug War

Margaret Haerens, Book Editor

GREENHAVEN PRESS
A part of Gale, Cengage Learning

GALE
CENGAGE Learning·

Detroit • New York • San Francisco • New Haven, Conn • Waterville, Maine • London

Elizabeth Des Chenes, *Director, Content Strategy*
Cynthia Sanner, *Publisher*
Douglas Dentino, *Manager, New Product*

For more information, contact:
Greenhaven Press
27500 Drake Rd.
Farmington Hills, MI 48331-3535
Or you can visit our Internet site at gale.cengage.com

Articles in Greenhaven Press anthologies are often edited for length to meet page require-ments. In addition, original titles of these works are changed to clearly present the main thesis and to explicitly indicate the author's opinion. Every effort is made to ensure that Greenhaven Press accurately reflects the original intent of the authors. Every effort has been made to trace the owners of copyrighted material.

Cover image © Images.com/Corbis.

LIBRARY OF CONGRESS CATALOGING-IN-PUBLICATION DATA

Mexico's drug war / Margaret Haerens, book editor.
    pages cm. -- (At issue)
   Includes bibliographical references and index.
   ISBN 978-0-7377-6844-2 (hardcover) -- ISBN 978-0-7377-6845-9 (pbk.)
   1. Drug traffic--Mexico--Juvenile literature. 2. Drug control--Mexico. 3. Drug traffic--Social aspects--Mexico--Juvenile literature. I. Haerens, Margaret, editor of compilation.
   HV5831.M46M48 2013
   363.450972--dc23
                                        2013009206

Printed in the United States of America
1 2 3 4 5 6 7 17 16 15 14 13

Contents

Introduction

The violent and often deadly conflicts between ruthless drug cartels operating in Mexico have shocked people around the world. The gruesome headlines and television footage of drug-related killings are enough to trouble any observer. Also worrisome to officials and experts, both in- and outside of Mexico, is the far-reaching impact of the drug war: the hundreds of thousands of cartel members involved in the illegal drug trade and resulting violence; the equal number of law enforcement officials, including local, regional, and federal forces assigned to drug enforcement duties; the nearly two million Mexican people displaced by the violence; and the approximately sixty thousand people, according to some estimates, killed by the ongoing conflict. The level of violence and brutality exhibited in the drug war is equally disturbing. Drug cartel members, law enforcement, government figures and policymakers, and innocent bystanders are viciously tortured, dismembered, beaten, and murdered in ways that have shocked even the most hardened law enforcement experts. The drug cartels have worked to eliminate or intimidate any threat, even high-level government authorities or powerful corporate figures. The threats of violence and widespread fear inspired by the cartels have functioned to destabilize Mexico's social, economic, and political systems and become a dire threat to its national security—and that of its powerful northern neighbor, the United States.

The root of Mexico's current crisis can be traced back through the country's history. Throughout the early twentieth century, Mexico cemented its place as a central shipping point for a variety of black market products destined for the United States. During Prohibition (1919–1933), Mexican bootleggers and organized criminals smuggled illegal liquor across the border into the United States. Once Prohibition was repealed and liquor was legal in America again, those smuggling routes were used for narcotics and other contraband. The flow of drugs through Mexico began to escalate with the popularity of heroin and marijuana in the 1960s, cocaine in the 1970s, and crack cocaine in the 1980s. Although much of the drug trade was controlled by powerful Colombian cartels, Mexican syndicates soon began to find ways to get in on the action, eventually gaining more traction in the business. In the early 1980s, a former federal police officer, Miguel Ángel Félix Gallardo ("The Godfather"), formed the first Mexican cartel, the Guadalajara Cartel, which dominated the illegal drug trade in Mexico and the smuggling of large amounts of cocaine and opium into the United States for years. He then divided up the drug trade between several Mexican cartels in order to avoid law enforcement and open up new opportunities.

Mexican politics also played a key role in the development of the drug cartels. After more than seventy years in power, the Institutional Revolutionary Party (PRI) was voted out of office in 2000. The political vacuum left by the once-dominant PRI was filled by ineffective or corrupt politicians and the drug cartels, who saw the opportunity to capitalize on the political instability and grab all the power they could. At stake was an estimated $25 billion a year industry: trafficking drugs into the United States. Politicians were threatened, corrupted, or assassinated. Innocent civilians were terrorized. Anyone who opposed the power grab was intimidated, brutalized, or killed. In many areas, drug cartels became the local power structure as Mexico's existing institutions were ill-equipped to stand up to these emerging threats effectively.

As drug cartels became more powerful, they began to fight each other for control over lucrative trafficking routes, drug supplies, and other valuable resources. In one major incident in late 2005, the Gulf and Sinaloa cartels waged a massive battle in Nuevo Laredo, a city under the control of the Gulf cartel. For months, the two cartels held massive shootouts on city streets and assassinated cartel members, government officials, law enforcement, and suspected opponents, keeping the city in the grip of terror. Reporters were bullied into silence under the threat of brutal retaliation.

The violence perpetrated by the drug cartels became a top issue in Mexico's 2006 elections. Felipe Calderón, the new president, vowed to confront the problem and launched Operation Michoacán, regarded as the government's first major operation against organized crime. Calderón sent 6,500 federal forces to the state of Michoacán, a region that was being torn apart by drug violence. He justified the use of federal troops by identifying the cartels as a national security risk. For many observers, it was also a recognition that many local police forces had been completely corrupted by the cartels' massive financial resources—a cash payoff could convince many police officers, who made a very low salary, to look the other way or even participate in cartel operations. Other local law enforcement departments just didn't have the resources to put up a decent fight against a well-financed and ruthless cartel.

From 2006 to 2012, Calderón employed more than fifty thousand federal troops in Mexico to fight the drug cartels. He also turned to the United States, who had come to believe that Mexico's drug violence posed a national security threat. With drug violence reportedly seeping into border cities and border patrol agents and other officials threatened by organized crime, the United States was willing to make a significant commitment to support Calderón's efforts.

Launched in 2008, the Merida Initiative is a US security effort to help fund the government's battle against the drug cartels. The US Congress approved a $465 million counterdrug assistance package for Mexico and Central American countries as well as state-of-the-art equipment, ranging from high-end helicopters to advanced surveillance hardware. The Merida Initiative also signaled US recognition that Mexico's drug wars were a shared problem, caused by America's insatiable hunger for illegal narcotics.

Critics of Calderón's military offensive against the cartels pointed to the widespread allegation of human rights abuses perpetrated by federal troops. A November 2011 report published by Human Rights Watch found that Calderón's public security policy "is badly failing on two fronts. It has not succeeded in reducing violence. Instead, it has resulted in a dramatic increase in grave human rights violations, virtually none of which appear to be adequately investigated. In sum, rather than strengthening public security in Mexico, Calderón's 'war' has exacerbated a climate of violence, lawlessness, and fear in many parts of the country" ("Neither Rights Nor Security," November 9, 2011).

By 2010, Calderón's efforts were widely recognized as a failure. Drug violence had escalated to unprecedented levels. Violent attacks on civilian populations continued unabated. Federal forces were accused of brutality and bold violations of human rights law. A number of high-level politicians were brazenly assassinated in public or just disappeared.

In the 2012 elections, Mexican voters returned power back to the PRI by electing a new president, Enrique Peña Nieto. During his campaign, Nieto promised to shift law enforcement focus from showy drug busts to a renewed offensive against smaller, local gangs that have terrorized communities by employing kidnapping and extortion as well as drug dealing. Nieto's election has sparked hope in many quarters that drug-related violence will drop and communities and local institutions will have the chance to stabilize without the threat of random and constant bloodshed.

This volume, *At Issue: Mexico's Drug War*, examines many relevant issues related to the conflict, including Mexico's reaction to the challenge and the US role in the problem, as well as its solution. The viewpoints collected here also discuss the value of the Merida Initiative, the impact of drug decriminalization on the illegal drug trade and drug violence, and the potential of Enrique Peña Nieto's new administration to effectively address the drug war in his country.

1

State of War

Sam Quinones

Sam Quinones is a reporter for the Los Angeles Times *and the author of two books on Mexico.*

Mexico's political instability has led to the rise of powerful and vicious drug cartels, who now fill the vacuum left by the demise of the country's one-party state led by the Institutional Revolutionary Party (PRI). The narcoculture in many parts of Mexico is so strong that it can be considered a threat to national security. With Mexico's institutions too weak to fight the cartels, the government turned to the military to address the problem with limited success. Until Mexico's cities have the power and funding to put a well-equipped and well-paid police force out on the streets, drug cartels will remain a dire threat to national security.

What I remember most about my return to Mexico last year are the narcomantas. At least that's what everyone called them: "drug banners." Perhaps a dozen feet long and several feet high, they were hung in parks and plazas around Monterrey. Their messages were hand-painted in black block letters. They all said virtually the same thing, even misspelling the same name in the same way. Similar banners appeared in eight other Mexican cities that day—Aug. 26, 2008.

The banners were likely the work of the Gulf drug cartel, one of the biggest drug gangs in Mexico. Its rival from the Pacific Coast, the Sinaloa cartel, had moved into Gulf turf near

Texas, and now the groups were fighting a propaganda war as well as an escalating gun battle. One banner accused the purported leader of the Sinaloa cartel, Joaquín "El Chapo" Guzmán Loera, of being protected by Mexican President Felipe Calderón and the army. After some time, the city's police showed up politely to take the banners down.

I'd recently lived in Mexico for a decade, but I'd never seen anything like this. I left in 2004—as it turned out, just a year before Mexico's long-running trouble with drug gangs took a dark new turn for the worse. Monterrey was the safest region in the country when I lived there, thanks to its robust economy and the sturdy social control of an industrial elite. The narcobanners were a chilling reminder of how openly and brazenly the drug gangs now operate in Mexico, and how little they fear the police and government.

That week in Monterrey, newspapers reported, Mexico clocked 167 drug-related murders. When I lived there, they didn't have to measure murder by the week. There were only about a thousand drug-related killings annually. The Mexico I returned to in 2008 would end that year with a body count of more than 5,300 dead. That's almost double the death toll from the year before—and more than all the U.S. troops killed in Iraq since that war began.

But it wasn't just the amount of killing that shocked me. When I lived in Mexico, the occasional gang member would turn up executed, maybe with duct-taped hands, rolled in a carpet, and dropped in an alley. But Mexico's newspapers itemized a different kind of slaughter last August: Twenty-four of the week's 167 dead were cops, 21 were decapitated, and 30 showed signs of torture. Campesinos found a pile of 12 more headless bodies in the Yucatán. Four more decapitated corpses were found in Tijuana, the same city where barrels of acid containing human remains were later placed in front of a seafood restaurant. A couple of weeks later, someone threw two hand grenades into an Independence Day celebration in Morelia, killing eight and injuring dozens more. And at any time, you could find YouTube videos of Mexican gangs executing their rivals—an eerie reminder of, and possibly a lesson learned from, al Qaeda in Iraq.

Then there are the guns. When I lived in Mexico, its cartels were content with assault rifles and large-caliber pistols, mostly bought at American gun shops. Now, Mexican authorities are finding arsenals that would have been incomprehensible in the Mexico I knew. The former U.S. drug czar, Gen. Barry McCaffrey, was in Mexico not long ago, and this is what he found:

> The outgunned Mexican law enforcement authorities face armed criminal attacks from platoon-sized units employing night vision goggles, electronic intercept collection, encrypted communications, fairly sophisticated information operations, sea-going submersibles, helicopters and modern transport aviation, automatic weapons, RPG's, Anti-Tank 66 mm rockets, mines and booby traps, heavy machine guns, 50 [caliber] sniper rifles, massive use of military hand grenades, and the most modern models of 40mm grenade machine guns.

These are the weapons the drug gangs are now turning against the Mexican government as Calderón escalates the war against the cartels.

Mexico's surge in gang violence has been accompanied by a similar spike in kidnapping. This old problem, once confined to certain unstable regions, is now a nationwide crisis. While I was in Monterrey, the supervisor of the city's office of the AFI—Mexico's FBI—was charged with running a kidnapping ring. The son of a Mexico City sporting-goods magnate was recently kidnapped and killed. Newspapers reported that women in San Pedro, once one of Mexico's safest cities, now take classes in surviving abductions.

All of this is taking a toll on Mexicans who had been insulated from the country's drug violence. Elites are retreating to bunkered lives behind video cameras and security gates. Others are fleeing for places like San Antonio and McAllen, Texas. Among them is the president of Mexico's prominent Grupo Reforma chain of newspapers. My week in Mexico last August ended with countrywide marches of people dressed in white, holding candles and demanding an end to the violence.

In Monterrey, most were from Mexico's middle and upper classes, people who view protests as the province of workers and radicals. In all my time in the country, I had seen such people turn to protest only once: during the 1994 peso crisis, when Mexico was on the brink of economic collapse.

I've traveled through most of Mexico's 31 states. I've written two books about the country. And yet I now struggle to recognize the place. Mexico is wracked by a criminal-capitalist insurgency. It is fighting for its life. And most Americans seem to have no idea what's happening right next door.

What happened in the four years I was gone? Fueled by American demand, dope was always there, of course. So was a surplus of weapons and gangs to use them. When I lived in Mexico, drug violence was a story, but not *the* story it is today.

I remember grander concerns back then: Mexico peacefully shedding 70 years of one-party authoritarian rule and dreaming of becoming a stable and prosperous democracy. But Mexico's one-party state, led by the Institutional Revolutionary Party (PRI), gave way to the control of a few parties, which were as inert and unaccountable as their authoritarian forebears. They bickered about minutiae in congress, and the hoped-for reforms didn't come. The PRI's centralized political control was gone, but nothing effectively took its place. This vacuum unleashed new opportunities for criminality, and Mexico's institutions weren't up to the new threats that emerged.

Most of the cartels that now battle for drug routes into the United States emerged in the Pacific Coast state of Sinaloa—a mid-sized Mexican state with an outsized drug problem. Mexican drug smuggling began primarily among rural and mountain people from lawless villages who are known to be especially *bronco*—wild. Marijuana and opium poppies grow easily in Sinaloa's hills. A narcoculture has evolved there, venerating smugglers and their swaggering hillbilly style, called *buchon*. Hicks became heroes. They moved into wealthy neighborhoods and fired guns in the air at parties. Bands sing their exploits; college kids know how they died. Sinaloa is that rare place where townies emulate hayseeds, and youths yearn to join their ranks.

Mexico's gangs had the means and motive to create upheaval, and in Mexico's failure to reform into a modern state, especially at local levels, the cartels found their opportunity.

These renegades have grown into a national security threat since I've been away from Mexico. One reason is that regional drug markets have changed a lot in the past few years. The Colombian government grew more successful against narcotraffickers who had taken over large parts of Colombia. Enforcement in the Caribbean also improved. Once-settled Mexican smuggling routes suddenly became the best way to move dope through Latin America and into the United States. Those routes were now up for grabs, and much more was at stake. Old gang enmities exploded. Mexico's cartels could not let their rivals take over new drug routes for fear they'd grow stronger. The gangs began vying for turf in an increasingly savage war with a constantly shifting front: Acapulco, Monterrey, Tijuana, Juárez, Nogales, and of course Sinaloa.

With war raging between Mexico's narcogangs, and with plenty of cash available from drug sales to Americans—$25 billion a year, by one reliable estimate—cartel gunmen began to grow discontented with the limited selection of arms found in the thousands of gun stores along the southern U.S. border.

Instead, they have sought out—and acquired—the world's fiercest weaponry. Today, hillbilly *pistoleros* are showing signs of becoming modern paramilitaries.

Mexico's gangs had the means and motive to create upheaval, and in Mexico's failure to reform into a modern state, especially at local levels, the cartels found their opportunity. Mexico has traditionally starved its cities. They have weak taxing power. Their mayors can't be reelected. Constant turnover breeds incompetence, improvisation, and corruption. Local cops are poorly paid, trained, and equipped. They have to ration bullets and gas and are easily given to bribery. Their morale stinks. So what should be the first line of defense against criminal gangs is instead anemic and easily compromised. Mexico has been left handicapped, and gangs that would have been stomped out locally in a more effective state have been able to grow into a powerful force that now attacks the Mexican state itself.

The first sign of trouble was Nuevo Laredo in late 2005. The Gulf and Sinaloa cartels staged street shootouts and midnight assassinations for months in this border city, which the Gulf cartel had controlled. One police chief lasted only hours from his swearing-in to his assassination. The state and municipal police took sides in the cartel fight. Newspapers had to stop reporting the news for fear of retaliation.

The problem isn't individuals; it's systemic.

Enter Calderón, who took office in late 2006, determined to address the growing war among Mexico's cartels. He broke with old half-measures of cargo takedowns that looked good but did little to damage the cartels. Calderón wanted arrests. He also began extraditing to the United States the *capos* and their lieutenants—more than 90 so far—who were already in custody and wanted up north.

But when Calderón looked across Mexico for allies to help him escalate the war on the narcogangs, he found few local governments and police forces that hadn't been starved to dysfunction. So he has had to rely on the only tool up to the task: Mexico's military. Calderón has also turned to the United States for help. The Merida Initiative, launched in April 2008, is a 10-fold increase in U.S. security assistance to a proposed $1.4 billion over several years, supplying Mexican forces with high-end equipment from helicopters to surveillance technology.

Fighting criminal gangs with a national military is an imperfect solution, but Calderón has scored some victories. He has captured or killed key gang leaders. Weapons seizures have been massive. Last November, the Mexican Army seized a house in Reynosa that contained the largest weapons cache ever found in the country, including more than 540 rifles, 500,000 rounds of ammunition, and 165 grenades.

Violence and criminality are moving north at a rapid pace.

The cartels have responded to Calderón's war with the kind of buchon savagery that so struck me upon returning to Mexico. In addition to fighting each other, the cartels are now increasingly fighting the Mexican state as well, and the killing shows no sign of slowing. The Mexican Army is outgunned, even with U.S. support. Calderón's purges of hundreds of public officials for corruption, cops among them, may look impressive, but they accomplish little. The problem isn't individuals; it's systemic. Until cities have the power and funding to provide strong and well-paid local police, Mexico's criminal gangs will remain a national threat, not a regional nuisance.

There's little reason to believe 2009 won't look a lot like 2008. And there's reason to fear it will be worse. The financial crisis is hitting Mexico hard. How long it can hang on is unclear. The momentum still favors the gangs, meaning the bloodshed will likely subside only when they tire of warring.

Americans watch this upheaval with curious detachment. One warning sign is Phoenix. This city has replaced Miami as the prime gateway for illegal drugs entering the United States. Cartel chaos in Mexico is pushing bad elements north along with the dope—enforcers without work and footloose to freelance.

Phoenix—the snowbird getaway, the land of yellow cardigans and emerald fairways—is now awash in kidnappings—366 in 2008 alone, up from 96 a decade ago. Most committing these crimes hail from Sinaloa, several hundred miles south. In one alarming incident, a gang of Mexican nationals, dressed in Phoenix police uniforms and using high-powered weapons and military tactics, stormed a drug dealer's house in a barrage of gunfire, killing him and taking his dope.

Phoenix is hanging tough—for now. Its capable local police, so desperately lacking in Mexico, are managing to quarantine the problem. No one unconnected to smuggling has been abducted, police say, and no kidnapping victim has been lost in a case they have been asked to investigate. As a result, most Phoenix residents live blithely unaware that hundreds of people in the smuggling underworld are kidnapped in their midst every year.

Still, violence and criminality are moving north at a rapid pace, and Americans would be foolhardy to imagine capable police departments like Phoenix's going for long without cracking under the pressure. As one Phoenix police officer told me, "Our fear is, we're going to meet our match."

2

Mexico's Criminal Justice System Is Too Weak to Stop the Drug Cartels

William Booth

William Booth is a correspondent for the Washington Post.

The 2009 arrest of ten mayors in Mexico for alleged ties to powerful drug cartels was initially hailed as a long-awaited success against corrupt politicians who had acted with impunity for years. When the cases against the mayors fell apart months later because of lack of evidence, observers began to question the arrests as political in nature and a cautionary tale about the deeply rooted problems in Mexico's ineffective criminal-justice system. The poor reputation of Mexico's criminal justice system prevails in spite of the considerable amounts of financial aid the United States has provided in recent years to help bolster the rule of law in the country.

When soldiers swarmed into city halls last year [2009] to arrest 10 mayors for alleged ties to an infamous drug cartel, Mexican authorities and their U.S. government allies boasted that the age of impunity for corrupt Mexican politicians was finally over.

The mass detentions of elected officials from bustling towns dominated the news in Mexico, and they were seen as a

William Booth, "Mexico Hobbled in Drug War by Arrests That Lead Nowhere," *Washington Post*, April 26, 2010, A1. Copyright © 2010 by the Washington Post. All rights reserved. Reproduced by permission.

bold new thrust in a vicious drug war that has left more than 22,000 dead as increasingly powerful drug cartels challenge the authority of the state.

A Cautionary Tale

But one by one, the government of President Felipe Calderón has quietly released the politicians as federal prosecutors dropped their cases and as judges ordered them set free for lack of evidence. U.S. diplomats who hailed the arrests now rarely mention them, except as a cautionary tale about how difficult it is to change Mexico's ineffective criminal-justice system.

The episode illustrates a central challenge faced by Mexico, where law enforcement authorities remain hard pressed to win major conspiracy cases, either because they arrest the wrong people or because prosecutors remain hobbled by incompetence.

It also suggests that despite Calderón's pledges of sweeping reform, Mexico has a long way to go in rebuilding its corrupt and hapless police and judiciary.

Nine of the 10 mayors arrested last May [2009] in the western state of Michoacan are now free. The latest was released Friday [April 23, 2010] after 11 months in prison. Most of them have returned to their duties at city hall, some after months of incarceration. Several mayors told *The Washington Post* that they were held in shackles for hours every day, kept in isolated units, and denied access to relatives and lawyers.

It is common in Mexico for drug suspects to be arrested with fanfare—and for their criminal cases to fall apart later.

None of the cases went to trial. No explanation has been issued, no apologies given. Another two mayors from Michoacan were arrested more recently and remain in jail, their fates unknown.

"I confess that when they arrested the mayors, myself and many people thought, finally!" said Miguel Sarre, a lawyer and professor at the Autonomous Technological Institute of Mexico and a leading expert on the nation's judiciary. "But this shows that either the government was not capable of thorough investigation and making a strong case, or the arrests were politically motivated." He noted that the mayors were incarcerated on the eve of midterm elections.

Problematic Arrests

It is common in Mexico for drug suspects to be arrested with fanfare—and for their criminal cases to fall apart later. But the arrests of the mayors, all accused of working for a gang of methamphetamine manufacturers and assassins known as La Familia, was hailed by U.S. officials and others as evidence of a new resolve on the part of Calderón's government. Calderón and his drug warriors, observers hoped, would move quickly to other states and attack what U.S. and Mexican experts say is at the core of organized crime in Mexico—a powerful nexus between corrupt politicians, crooked cops and millionaire criminals. Calderón's government did not arrest politicians in other states.

"They claimed I had received funds during my election campaign from organized-crime groups and that in return I was providing with them protection," said José Cortés Ramos, the mayor of Aquila, Michoacan, who was released after a month in prison. He asked, "How could we offer protection?" His local police "don't even have the guns they need," he said.

"I think that the federal government's operations against organized crime aren't a bad thing," Cortés said. "They are good. But we don't see any results. We don't see any results because the number of violent shootouts and killings isn't going down. Just the opposite."

Several of the arrested mayors belonged to Calderón's own center-right National Action Party, and Michoacan is the state where Calderón was born and raised, where he launched the military against the cartels in December 2006.

"There was immediately a perception that the arrests were politically motivated," said David A. Shirk, a specialist on Mexico's judiciary who directs the Trans-Border Institute at the University of San Diego. "It looked suspicious, coming right before the elections, but the government was given the benefit of the doubt, because of the level of threat they face from organized crime."

The Mexican legislature gave the government new legal tools to prosecute organized-crime cases, allowing the state to hold suspects for almost three months without charges and to use testimony from confidential informants and government wiretaps.

Mexico's War on Drugs

In 2008, at the urging of the United States, the Mexican legislature gave the government new legal tools to prosecute organized-crime cases, allowing the state to hold suspects for almost three months without charges and to use testimony from confidential informants and government wiretaps.

"But the fact that they couldn't build a case against the mayors, it looks bad," Shirk said. "It really shows the challenges Mexico faces, and how law enforcement has to become much better at what it does."

For its part, the U.S. government is spending $1.3 billion in its Merida Initiative aid package: attempting to bolster the rule of law in Mexico by employing FBI instructors to train federal police detectives at a new academy and by sending Mexican prosecutors to U.S. classrooms in hopes of transforming the judiciary. The [Barack] Obama administration has asked Congress for another $310 million for 2011.

"The cartels never pressured me to cooperate. They never called me," said Antonio González, a Xerox dealer and mayor of Uruapan, a bustling city in the heart of Michoacan's avocado country.

During his eight months in jail, González said, investigators told him that they had been listening in on his phone calls for six months. "I kept waiting to see some evidence of my crime," said González, who spent the days jumping an imaginary rope and working on his memoirs.

González recalls being shoved by masked federal agents into helicopters and buses. "'Here comes another package. Just another package,' they yelled. And in that moment I was no longer a person but a package," he said, "I wasn't Antonio González any longer. I was a package."

He said the accusations against him came from anonymous tips. "My lawyers told me: 'This is a joke. Any lawyer can see that they don't have any evidence against you. There's no way you'll even spend the 40 days here. You should be out in a couple of days,'" said González, who belongs to Calderón's party.

He says he was interrogated by a prosecutor who badgered him to confess that he once had lunch with a cartel member named "Mr. Gómez," whom González says he does not remember.

"This was all based in rumors. Rumors and lies. They were looking for a scapegoat and people talk, perhaps for political reasons," González said. "It was a horrible experience, just horrible."

An Abuse of Power?

Mexican prosecutors declined to discuss the mayors' cases.

"The government is abusing its use of secrecy," said Arturo Hernández, the attorney for González. "This is a time in which we're seeing an excessive use of force by the authorities. There is an exaggerated psychological pressure on detainees: People are not allowed to speak to their families or attorneys. They pressure you to admit to the charges against you."

Leonel Godoy Rangel, governor of Michoacan, complained that the federal government treated the mayors like criminals but acted with little evidence; he said the mayors deserve an apology.

Interior Secretary Fernando Gómez-Mont said no apology will be forthcoming. The mayors were released because judges found insufficient evidence, he said, not because "their innocence has been proven."

3

Mexico's Military Response to Drug Violence Is Not Working

Nik Steinberg

Nik Steinberg is a researcher in the Americas division of Human Rights Watch.

As drug cartel violence has swept through Mexico, political leaders and policymakers have turned to the military as the only law enforcement institution powerful enough to combat the grip of the drug cartels. However, violence has increased significantly in the seven states where the military has been deployed and investigations into drug violence have floundered. The military has shut out local authorities and charges of human rights violations perpetrated by soldiers have skyrocketed. As a result, the military has alienated communities whose cooperation is essential to combat the drug cartels.

The first one appeared on February 3, 2010, before sunrise. It hung from the statue of José Maria Morelos that faces the colonial statehouse at the center of Monterrey. Morelos was a priest turned revolutionary leader in Mexico's war of independence, and the large white sheet bearing a message from a drug cartel spanned the entire length of the hero's bronze horse. Here Comes the Monster, it read, and was signed "Z." That same morning, six similar handwritten messages, also signed "Z," appeared in the municipalities surrounding Monterrey. Soldiers came, removed them and drove off.

The *narcomantas*, as these public communiqués of the cartels are known, presaged a horrific explosion of violence in Monterrey, a city of 4 million people in northeastern Mexico and the country's financial capital. In the months that followed, students would be gunned down at the gate of the city's elite university. A mayor would be abducted, tortured and murdered. City squares, police stations and even the US consulate would be attacked with grenades. Blockades controlled by masked gunmen would paralyze the city for days on end. At the root of this violence was a turf war between the authors of the *narcomantas*, the Zetas, and their former ally the Gulf Cartel.

Monterrey Quickly Becomes Chaotic

It was the kind of violence one had come to expect in places like Ciudad Juárez or Tijuana—border cities that have long served as trafficking hubs to the United States. But how could thriving Monterrey, the "Sultan of the North," which only years earlier had been deemed one of the safest cities in Latin America, descend so quickly into chaos? If it could happen here, was anywhere in Mexico safe for long?

> *Conducting illicit business in someone else's plaza without permission is tantamount to declaring war.*

Yet what from the outside looked like a sudden collapse was in reality decades in the making. At its root was the decay of the institutions entrusted with providing law and order, ones that, despite their chronic dysfunction and corruption, had been able to contain drug violence in the old state-run system. But when that system crumbled, and when, in the face of "the monster" of organized crime, Monterrey's elite, politicians and public turned to those institutions to rescue them, they found them rotten to the core. And so, Monterrey's residents turned in desperation to the last power they felt they could trust: the military. It was a choice many would come to regret.

The Symbolic Plaza Is Run by a Drug Cartel

Every city and town in Mexico has a plaza. It's where candidates are sworn in and protests staged, where concerts are held and local heroes memorialized. Kids congregate there after school, couples stroll there on dates and old men hold court over worn chessboards. The plaza is invariably flanked by a church and the local seat of government, which speaks to the importance of these institutions in Mexicans' lives.

In the early twentieth century a different kind of plaza emerged—a symbolic one, with its boundaries encompassing the territory run by a drug cartel. To own it is to control trafficking and distribution in a given area—a highly profitable and, as a result, fiercely contested business. This plaza can span a few city blocks or can span several states. Regardless of its size, a plaza is acquired and maintained through violence. Conducting illicit business in someone else's plaza without permission is tantamount to declaring war.

What control by the PRI governments guaranteed was that drug trafficking did not disturb the societal peace.

Until recently, nobody ran the plaza—or any other legitimate or illegitimate business—without the tacit permission of the Institutional Revolutionary Party (PRI). In what has been dubbed "the perfect dictatorship," the PRI ruled Mexico continuously for more than seventy years, beginning in 1930. While Mexico under the PRI appeared to be an electoral democracy, politicians tapped their successors and power flowed vertically from the president all the way down to the lowest bureaucrat. The president even handpicked his heir every six years in a ritual known as the *dedazo*, or big finger.

The PRI's control extended far beyond politics to everything from industrial development to land reform. All business was controlled by a patronage system, which enriched politicians and their allies and perpetually tightened the party's grip on power. Working outside the system, let alone trying to remake it, was unthinkable.

Drug trafficking was no exception. By and large the PRI turned a blind eye to the illicit trade, so long as the cartels gave government officials a cut of the profits and prevented the violence from spilling into the traditional plaza. The authorities responsible for regulating the drug trade—initially health officials, and later the police and the military—often functioned as middlemen between politicians and traffickers. Every so often, a high-profile arrest was made to appease the United States, which was constantly pressing for more aggressive enforcement. Luis Astorga, a historian of the drug trade, has written that in the rare instances when the police and military intervened, it was to prevent "traffickers from becoming completely autonomous or getting so wild as to go beyond certain limits of socially and historically tolerated violence." Or, as Nuevo León's governor from the early 1990s would later put it, "What control by the PRI governments guaranteed was that drug trafficking did not disturb the societal peace."

The Mexican government says that in the past four years [2007–2010] it has recovered 60,000 guns traceable to dealers in the United States.

The Implications of Political Change

The unraveling of that order began with a seismic political shift. In 2000 Vicente Fox, of the National Action Party (PAN), was elected Mexico's first non-PRI president since 1930. The

PRI also lost several key governorships that year. One of the perverse consequences of this democratic opening was to upset the balance that had, for decades, limited competition among drug cartels and their political allies. Local power brokers were suddenly free to negotiate their own arrangements, whether by forging new deals with rival groups or by taking a more aggressive line on enforcement. The result was greater fluidity in the alliances between politicians, security forces and criminal groups.

At the same time, Mexico's cartels were evolving from national drug trafficking organizations to transnational organized crime syndicates. They diversified the drugs they traded (for instance, their production of methamphetamines increased) and branched out into other illicit activities, including extortion, kidnapping and human trafficking. As the groups sought out new markets and territory, they increasingly came into greater competition with one another and the political proxies who gave them protection.

It was also during the Fox administration that the US ban on assault weapons expired. Beginning in 2004, high-powered firearms could once again be purchased easily in states like Texas and Arizona, transported with little effort across the porous border and sold at inflated prices to criminals in Mexico. Not surprisingly, organized crime groups were soon running the North-to-South weapons trade as well. The Mexican government says that in the past four years [2007–2010] it has recovered 60,000 guns traceable to dealers in the United States.

Monterrey is the capital of Nuevo León, and until recently its plaza was controlled exclusively by the Gulf Cartel, which got its start in the 1970s. In the futile scenario of whack-a-mole [phrase deriving from an arcade game that means to engage in a repetitious, futile battle] that is the history of US counternarcotics efforts, the Gulf Cartel's breakthrough came in the late 1980s, when a massive crackdown by the US government on drugs flowing through Miami led Colombian cartels to reroute much of the cocaine trade through Mexico. The Gulf Cartel emerged as one of the key middlemen between Colombian producers and American buyers, and it came to dominate the trafficking route in the three states along Mexico's eastern border with the United States: Tamaulipas, Coahuila and Nuevo León. . . .

A Brutal Turf Battle

Across Nuevo León and Tamaulipas, the respective strongholds of the Zetas and the Gulf Cartel, high-power firefights erupted along main thoroughfares, and mutilated bodies were displayed like trophies in public squares. As shocking to Nuevo León's residents as the explosion of violence was the authorities' powerlessness to stop it. In April [2011] the tortured body of a policeman was dumped in Santiago, a municipality near Monterrey. A handwritten letter attached to his chest listed the names of thirty-five police officers who, the letter alleged, worked for the Zetas. There were X's next to four names, all of them police officers who had been killed in previous weeks. The list was signed by the Gulf Cartel, together with the Familia Michoacana and the Sinaloa Cartel, groups with traditional strongholds in other states. (Cartels are fluid and opportunistic by nature, and it is not uncommon for them to form alliances to win one plaza while fighting over another.)

The traditional order had been upended. Now organized crime was establishing boundaries for the authorities, not the other way around.

While some police were targeted because of their ties to a cartel, others were singled out for trying to do their job. Monterrey's mayor responded by trying to clean up the transit department, because its role in screening commerce crossing the state made it particularly susceptible to collusion with cartels. The mayor appointed Enrique Barrios transit secretary in May 2010 and ordered him to investigate the department's ties to organized crime. Barrios created an internal affairs department, with four lawyers who would report directly to him.

All four were kidnapped in their first two weeks on the job. Barrios's second-in-command was abducted next. They came for Barrios several hours before daybreak; so certain was he of his fate that, when he heard someone breaking in, he got out of bed, went to his window and yelled, "I'm coming!" He walked to the front door and turned himself over to his abductors, asking only that they spare his family. He was released days later, badly beaten, and resigned shortly thereafter. He has remained silent about the episode.

During the Calderón administration's tenure, Mexico's National Human Rights Commission has received nearly 5,000 allegations of grave human rights abuses committed by the army.

The message sent by abductions like that of Barrios—and there were many, the victims of which were politicians, police, the business elite and their families—was clear. The traditional order had been upended. Now organized crime was establishing boundaries for the authorities, not the other way around. That more than one criminal group was setting the rules and demanding allegiance only complicated matters. Staying neutral was unacceptable, but choosing the wrong side could be deadly. . . .

A Failed Strategy?

In August 2010 Monterrey's major newspapers ran a full-page advertisement from the city's business elite that took the form of an open letter to President Felipe Calderón and Nuevo León's governor. "Enough already," the letter said. It called on the president to dispatch four additional military battalions—

roughly 2,400 more troops—to Nuevo León. In a roundabout way, the letter was an endorsement of Calderón's public-security strategy, announced days after he took office in December 2006, of deploying the military to take on the drug cartels. By the time Monterrey's business leaders published their letter, Calderón had dispatched more than 45,000 troops in counternarcotics operations across the country.

After four years, however, there are serious reasons to doubt whether Calderón's strategy is working. Violence has increased significantly in all seven states where the military is deployed against drug cartels, including Nuevo León. A recent study found that homicide rates in these states are nearly double what had previously been the record over the past two decades. Defending his strategy in the face of rising violence, Calderón has said, "If you see dust in the air, it's because we're cleaning house." He has repeatedly claimed that 90 percent of the victims of drug violence are criminals, yet he has provided no supporting data. A freedom of information request made last June [2010] by a Mexican newspaper revealed that federal prosecutors had opened only 1,200 investigations into drug-related crimes during his administration, while nearly 23,000 Mexicans had been killed in drug-related violence. (The most recent estimate of deaths is 35,000.)

The increasing role of the military in public-security operations is part of the reason investigations are not opened. In states like Nuevo León, the military functions as a shadow police force. Soldiers carry out regular patrols, man checkpoints and respond to shootouts. Local newspapers run advertisements for military hot lines, which citizens can call to report anonymously on suspicious activity. When it comes to working with civilian authorities, however, the military sets the terms. As Nuevo León's ranking military officer said in a recent meeting with civil society leaders, "We work with civilian authorities when we have to—when there are levels of trust. If not, we work alone." When I met with the governor's senior staff, they conceded that they had no control over the timing or location of military operations, and a police chief in Monterrey said the army did not notify him when it carried out raids.

Allegations of Human Rights Violations in Mexico

Given the high levels of corruption among local authorities, the military's reluctance to collaborate is understandable. Yet its tendency to operate autonomously often translates into soldiers' assuming roles for which they have not been trained—such as collecting evidence at crime scenes or interrogating suspects. As the military has assumed such roles, civilian complaints of human rights violations by soldiers have skyrocketed. During the Calderón administration's tenure, Mexico's National Human Rights Commission has received nearly 5,000 allegations of grave human rights abuses committed by the army, including rape, torture and extra-judicial killings. In Nuevo León, Human Rights Watch investigated eight killings in 2010 that evidence indicates were the result of the military's unlawful use of lethal force.

One was the case of a married couple, Juan Carlos Peña Chavarria and Rocio Romeli Elias Garza, both 29, who lived in Anáhuac, north of Monterrey. During their lunch break on March 3, 2010, the couple left the factory where they worked and got caught in a shootout between the military and armed men. When the shooting tapered off, Peña tried to run for safety. He was shot by soldiers, two witnesses told me. Elias raised her hands, yelled that they were unarmed civilians and pleaded for help. She was shot by a soldier standing about ten feet away. Soldiers shot her and Peña again, at point-blank range, and planted weapons near their bodies. The military released a statement the following day saying it had killed eight criminals in a shootout, including Peña and Elias.

Incidents like the killing of Peña and Elias have ripple effects, alienating communities whose cooperation is critical for an effective counternarcotics campaign. Time and again, victims' families, neighbors and co-workers told me they had welcomed the military's intervention in Nuevo León until they were personally affected by its brutality. "I used to believe in the army," said the mother of a 22-year-old who disappeared in 2010 after being detained by the military. "Now I only believe in God."

The Nuevo León government has realized that if it is to address the city's rampant violence, it needs to win back neighborhoods like Independencia.

Independencia Was Taken Over by Gangs

Independencia's poverty has made it fertile recruiting ground for criminal groups. Of the estimated 35,000 gang members in the greater Monterrey area—a figure that tripled from 2006 to 2009—the majority come from Independencia. And as the violence has increased, Independencia has become the exclusive turf of gangs, a place for them to store drugs, arms, even people. (Trafficking undocumented migrants and sex workers is among the cartels' most profitable trades.) Police rarely dare to go there.

One police officer I met described getting lost in Independencia's labyrinthine streets. He was leading a small detail providing security for a politician who was visiting the neighborhood. Suddenly, he said, he looked up to see a group of more than a dozen teenagers, all masked and armed with AK-47s, hovering on the rooftops. "I was sure we were dead," the officer said. As the police wound their way out of the maze the teens kept their weapons trained on them, hopping from roof to roof.

A New Strategy Targets Poverty

The Nuevo León government has realized that if it is to address the city's rampant violence, it needs to win back neighborhoods like Independencia. As part of a new strategy often called "reconstructing the social fabric," it is initiating projects to tackle the poverty that leads many people to crime. In addition to beefing up security, these programs aim at investing in healthcare, education and job training in the most marginalized communities. Similar projects have been initiated in cities like Ciudad Juárez and Tijuana.

The office of Nuevo León's governor, Rodrigo de la Cruz, agreed to take me to Independencia to show me the pilot project. My guide was Edgar Oláiz, who directs the project, and we met in his office on the second floor of the ornate statehouse. Before we left, he clicked through a PowerPoint presentation that outlined the city's plans for investing roughly $14 million in the project to "prevent 8- to 13-year-olds from joining cartels." One slide showed an overhead map of metropolitan Monterrey, with red dots marking locations where violent crimes had occurred. Clusters of red filled Independencia's hills.

After the slide show, we piled into an unmarked armored Suburban. From behind a pair of aviator glasses the driver clenched his jaw as we crossed over the Santa Catarina riverbed and worked our way uphill into Independencia, cursing under his breath at any obstacle that forced him to slow down.

It Will Take Years to Fix Problems

We stopped first at the school complex, at the heart of what will be a renovated community center. It was a little after noon on a Monday, but the classrooms were empty. A caretaker lumbered over to meet us, and Oláiz asked where the director had gone. "Home," the caretaker said. Oláiz looked disappointed but decided to give the tour himself. The courtyard between the school buildings was overgrown with tall grasses and littered with garbage bags and chunks of concrete. Workers had applied a fresh coat of lime-green paint to one building; the others were covered in graffiti. "That will be a workshop to train machinists," Oláiz said, pointing to a gutted building nearby. He saw me looking at the charred remains of a recent fire on the ground. "The gangs sometimes congregate here at night," he added. As we walked across a lot where bulldozers were leveling earth, Oláiz gestured to a cluster of buildings on the hillside above us. "Those are *casas de sequridad* [safe houses], where the kidnappers keep their victims while they demand a ransom. We don't go up there."

A stout woman with short brown hair walked swiftly over to us, shaking hands with Oláiz and introducing herself to me. She had been a community organizer for the PRI, the governor's party, for decades. She said that as recently as a few years ago, drugs in Independencia were sold in small quantities by grandmothers who ran corner stores. Then, she said, a group arrived and told everyone that they now controlled business in the area. They drove around in new SUVs with tinted windows. "Zetas," she said. She indicated an abandoned police outpost fifty yards away. "They took over that too."

As we spoke, an elderly man walked by, leading a donkey by the reins up the hill. Cases of Coca-Cola, cans of tomatoes, bags of rice and other basic supplies were secured by a mess of rope to the beast's back. I asked the woman where he was headed. "Him?" She laughed. "He's a *burrero*—a donkey taxi! It's how we get supplies up the hill." As we drove back toward Monterrey, I asked Oláiz how long it would take to fix the problems in places like Independencia that were behind Monterrey's crime. "Years," he said. "The system's been broken a long time." Did they have years to spare? There was a long pause. "What other option do we have?" he asked.

4

Corruption, Drug Cartels, and the Mexican Police

Ted Galen Carpenter

Ted Galen Carpenter is an author and senior fellow at the Cato Institute.

A series of recent attacks on US government personnel stationed in Mexico has cast a light on the troubling corruption of the Mexican military and law enforcement by the drug cartels that operate throughout the country. In an attack on August 24, 2012, it appears that the perpetrators are members of Mexico's federal police force. Infiltration of Mexican law enforcement at all levels is a crippling obstacle to fighting the cartels and poses a huge security problem for the United States.

On August 24, an armored U.S. embassy SUV was attacked in the mountains south of Mexico City. Gunmen pursued the vehicle at high speeds, riddling it with bullets and wounding two of the occupants. Now the mysterious attack has become even more troubling.

It was the fourth significant attack in the past few years on U.S. government personnel stationed in Mexico. In March 2010, Lesley Enriquez Redelfs, an employee of the U.S. consulate in Ciudad Juárez, was shot to death in her car along with her husband, Arthur, in broad daylight after leaving a children's party sponsored by the U.S. consul. The husband of another consular employee was killed and their two children seriously wounded on the same day in a separate drive-by shooting. Jaime Zapata, a special U.S. Immigration and Customs Enforcement agent on assignment to the U.S. embassy in Mexico City, suffered a similar fate in February 2011. Zapata and another ICE agent were returning to the capital after meeting with law-enforcement officials in the northern state of San Luis Potosi when they were ambushed.

But while those previous attacks clearly were carried out by hitmen employed by the violent Mexican drug cartels, the perpetrators of this assault appear to be twelve members of Mexico's federal police. The circumstances of the pursuit and attack seem to rule out the scenario of mistaken identity. Although the exact reason for the attack has yet to be established, the most likely explanation is that the incident is the latest case of penetration of Mexico's police forces by the cartels. Indeed, the *New York Times* reports that the "embassy personnel" in the SUV were CIA agents assisting the Mexican Navy in antidrug efforts, giving the cartels an obvious motive for ordering an attack. And the *Washington Post* quotes President Felipe Calderón as believing that the federal police involved had "ties to criminal organizations."

It would certainly not be the first high-profile case of supposed law-enforcement personnel doing the bidding of the criminal syndicates. It is a long-standing problem. In February 2000, Tijuana's police chief was assassinated, and a short time later, seven men, including two former members of the Tijuana police force, were arrested for the chief's killing. The men confessed to working for the Sinaloa cartel. In another incident, a bloody gun battle ensued in downtown Tijuana when police attempted to stop a drug trafficker's armed motorcade. The commander of the police unit and three officers were killed by the trafficker's bodyguards. Those bodyguards, it turned out, were local police officers.

The administration of President Vicente Fox (2000–2006) made a valiant effort to crack down on police who had been co-opted by the drug cartels. At one point, more than seven hundred officers were charged with offenses ranging from taking bribes to drug-related kidnapping and murder. Yet those arrested represented only the tip of a very big iceberg of corruption.

Both violence and police corruption in Nuevo Laredo reached the point in June 2005 that Mexico's national government suspended the city's police force and sent in the federal police to patrol the streets. Federal authorities proceeded to purge the local police, eventually firing 305 of the 765 police officers—forty-one of them for attacking the federal police when those units arrived in the city.

The corruption in Mexico's police forces runs very deep, and it grows steadily worse.

Matters across the country have not improved since then. In July 2009, nearly eighty police officers were arrested in eighteen towns across the state of Nuevo León after soldiers found their names on an organizational roster captured from traffickers. Just before Christmas of that year, soldiers discovered a list of dozens of police in Monterrey, Mexico's leading economic city, who were apparently on the payroll of traffickers—in some cases working as hit men.

Edelmiro Cavazos, the mayor of Santiago, a quaint tourist town a few hours from the U.S. border, certainly discovered that he could not trust his own police force. On the night of August 15, 2010, Cavazos was abducted from his home while his wife and children were visiting relatives in Texas. Two days later, his corpse was found dumped by the side of a road. He became one of fourteen mayors killed in 2010, but his murder was not the only awful aspect of the episode.

The security surveillance system showed one of the police officers assigned to guard the mayor's house walking out to meet an approaching convoy of cars. Armed men emerged from those vehicles and walked up to the front door. When Cavazos answered the door, the gunmen threatened him with drawn weapons, forced him outside and pushed him into the back seat of the lead vehicle. The subsequent investigation implicated the guard and five other officers for involvement in Cavazos' kidnapping and assassination.

Given that track record, it would not come as a great surprise if the investigation of the recent attack on the U.S. embassy employees shows that the federal police were doing the bidding of one of the cartels. The corruption in Mexico's police forces runs very deep, and it grows steadily worse.

Nor is the situation with the country's military much better. It should be remembered that the notorious Zetas cartel began in the late 1990s as a specially trained elite commando unit of the Mexican military. Indeed, the United States provided much of the training of that unit at Fort Bragg, North Carolina. Most of the individuals who have joined the Zetas in the intervening years are former police or military personnel.

The harsh truth is that Mexico's drug cartels are becoming stronger and more dangerous, and the law-enforcement and security agencies arrayed against them are riddled with turncoats and infiltrators. That is not surprising, since the drug syndicates have an estimated $35 billion to $60 billion a year in income at their disposal. Such a vast sum gives them an enormous capability to corrupt those people who are assigned to oppose them. The United States faces an increasingly troubling security situation on its southern border.

5

The Mexican Government's Drug Strategy Violates Civil Liberties

Laura Carlsen

Laura Carlsen is the director of the Americas Program at the Center for International Policy.

To combat the violence unleashed by powerful drug cartels, the Mexican government has deployed more than forty-five thousand military troops into various regions of the country. Critics of this campaign have charged that putting the military in charge of domestic law enforcement is against the rule of law and violates civil liberties. Soldiers have been accused of arbitrary arrests, torture, rape, excessive use of force, and extrajudicial executions. Prosecutions of crimes perpetrated by members of the military are rare because they are exempt from civil prosecutions. This lack of legal and social responsibility has led human rights activists to turn to international courts to address the growing problem.

Mexico is currently confronting a human rights crisis. Headlines document the overt violence that has claimed more than 50,000 lives since December 11, 2006 when President Felipe Calderón launched the war on drugs. Yet beneath the bloodshed, the erosion of the rule of law and the systematic violation of human rights in the context of the armed conflict caused by the drug war has created a more profound crisis in Mexican society, one whose causes and effects are not only ill-defined but often purposely obscured.

The War on Drugs and National Security

The war on drugs began with the premise that drug trafficking cartels presented the gravest threat to Mexican security and would therefore be a top priority of the incoming Calderón administration. The chosen strategy was modeled on the drug war devised by U.S. President Richard Nixon in 1971 that prioritized enforcement of laws prohibiting the sale and consumption of certain drugs at home, harsh criminalization of consumers and vendors, and interdiction strategies in producing nations. In a series of "Joint Operations" between Federal Police and Armed Forces, the Mexican government has deployed more than 45,000 troops into various regions of the country in an unprecedented domestic low-intensity conflict.

This deployment has raised numerous constitutional questions. Although there are some specific circumstances in which the use of the Mexican Armed Forces is considered justified within national territory, Article 129 of the Mexican Constitution restricts the functions of the Armed Forces in peace times to those directly connected to military discipline, and Article 21 stipulates that public security is the task of civil authorities. The federal government continues to define a semipermanent role for the Armed Forces in the drug war, which in the absence of a declared state of emergency is difficult to justify. Moreover, the domestic role of the Armed Forces threatens civil liberties and individual human rights and constitutes an affront to the rule of law.

This situation is compounded by the actions of the Armed Forces. Although trained in a war model that posits annihilation of an identifiable enemy, when deployed to communities where civilians are defined as suspected enemies, soldiers and officers have responded too often with arbitrary arrests, personal agendas and corruption, extrajudicial executions, the use of torture, and excessive use of force. The persistence of trying all cases related to military personnel in military tribunals, known as the *fuero militar* or military exemption from civil prosecution, inhibits legal and social accountability and in practice has led to a very low prosecution rate.

The National Commission on Human Rights (NCHR), HRW, and local and state human rights groups report major increases in forced disappearances, torture and extrajudicial executions, many allegedly perpetrated by Mexican security forces.

Human Rights Watch (HRW) reports that of 3,671 investigations opened in the military court system between 2007 and 2011, only 29 resulted in convictions of soldiers. In November 2009, the Inter-American Court of Human Rights (IACHR) mandated proscription of the use of military jurisdiction in cases involving human rights violations of civilians [*Radilla Pacheco v. Mexico*]. In a historic ruling, the Mexican Supreme Court held on July 6, 2011 that the armed forces must respect the decision of the IACHR. Despite the combined mandate of both the international and national ruling, in practice citizens must file for an injunction against trial in military courts on a case-by-case basis in order to demand investigation and trial in civilian courts.

Court Challenges

The first case to challenge military immunity won a decision by the Sixth District Court of the Second Region to an injunction against the extension of military immunity in the case on December 9, 2011. The family of Bonfilio Rubio Villegas, an indigenous Nahua man shot to death at a military checkpoint in the state of Guerrero, filed the case. Judge Carlos Alfredo Soto Morales ruled on the basis of the Constitution and cited the *Radilla* case, noting that rulings by the IACHR are binding under Mexican jurisprudence. After the federal court ruled that the Bonfilio Rubio Villegas case must be tried in a civil court the Army appealed the ruling, sparking protests by citizen organizations and experts that cited a continued resistance on the part of the Armed Forces to submit to civilian justice.

The National Commission on Human Rights (NCHR), HRW, and local and state human rights groups report major increases in forced disappearances, torture and extrajudicial executions, many allegedly perpetrated by Mexican security forces. There has been a 70 percent increase in complaints of human rights violations between 2010–2011 compared to the previous level, the majority of which were filed registered against security forces, especially the Federal Police and Army. The top categories are arbitrary arrest, torture, and extortion. On an official visit to Mexico, the U.N. [United Nations] High Commissioner of Human Rights, Navi Pillay, expressed grave concern over the militarization and expanded use of pre-trial house arrest; five U.N. bodies have recommended elimination of the practice as a violation of presumed innocence. The Mexican government has refused to reform the law or practice. The *Second Report on the Situation of Human Rights Defenders in the Americas* of the IACHR documented 61 murders of defenders in Mexico during the drug war period 2006–2010, and the National Network of Women Human Rights Defenders reports 17 female human rights defenders murdered from 2010 to date. Another report documents dozens of attacks on female human rights defenders, many including gender-based forms of violence.

The NCHR has registered 475 forced disappearances in September 2011, compared to some four to six cases in 2006. Especially in disappearances, cases are widely underreported. Human Rights Ombudsman Raúl Plascencia noted that the federal government does not register forced disappearances, nor are they investigated in most cases. The NCHR has begun a registry and investigations, but has not reached full coverage and the federal government approved a measure to begin a registry.

Because of the explosive increase in violence and human rights violations under the enforcement/interdiction drug war model, Mexican human rights groups and citizen organizations have demanded an immediate change in the security strategy.

Legal Gaps

Moreover, some major violations of human rights cannot be successfully prosecuted due to gaps in the law. Neither femicide, which has risen notably during the drug war period, nor forced disappearances are typified as such under the law. Currently femicides and disappearances are registered as kidnappings or missing person reports. As a result, the kidnapping unit of the Attorney General's Office (PGR) is overwhelmed and forced disappearances are not counted. Forced disappearances are not classified as a specific crime under Mexican federal law. Some Mexican states are thus moving to pass specific laws on forced disappearances and human rights groups in Mexico have called for a national law as well.

According to the Ministry of Defense, the Army receives an average of four human rights complaints a day as a result of its involvement in the drug war. The total number of complaints registered by the NCHR against the army since the start of the drug war under the Calderón administration is 5,055 by mid-2011; only 79 recommendations have been issued. The Ministry of Defense has attempted to minimize the gravity of this situation, stating that due to its offensive against organized crime, "there are complaints that are presented by members of organized crime to defame this armed institute and therefore limit its operations." However, this claim has not been substantiated, and investigations of most complaints are considerably delayed or limited. There is every reason to view with alarm the number of government statements that associate complaints of human rights violations with links to drug trafficking, as they point to an attitude of tainting or criminalizing human rights defenders, which puts them in greater jeopardy.

The precipitous rise in violence and human rights violations and the dysfunctional nature of the Mexican justice system have led directly to the filing and acceptance of numerous cases by international courts.

Paradigms for Security: The National Security Law and Citizen Security

Because of the explosive increase in violence and human rights violations under the enforcement/interdiction drug war model, Mexican human rights groups and citizen organizations have demanded an immediate change in the security strategy. The Movement for Peace with Justice and Dignity (MPJD), led by the poet Javier Sicilia whose son was brutally murdered in March of 2011, has formally called for an end to Calderón's drug war, a halt to the U.S.-funded Merida Initiative and rejection of the administration's proposed reforms to the National Security Law. The 2005 National Security Law places national security as the priority, and defines national security in Article 3: "For the effects of this Law, national security is understood as the actions destined to immediately and directly maintain the integrity, stability and permanence of the Mexican State. . . ."

The proposed reforms presented by President Calderón are aimed at institutionalizing the drug war model within this concept of national security and providing a stronger legal basis for the participation of the Armed Forces in the country. MPJD legal experts have criticized the 2005 National Security Law for the following reasons:

1. It legalizes presidential decisions to attack insecurity with repressive measures that react to symptoms rather than address causes.

2. It is unconstitutional since it redistributes public security and national security functions among the Armed Forces and the police without adequately defining both.

3. The Armed Forces would be allowed to coordinate public safety activities when the constitution clearly only allows them to participate as auxiliaries in crisis situations.

4. The incorporation of military personnel in public safety opens the door to substitute local and state authorities for federal Armed Forces and security personnel, which affects states' rights and sovereignty.

5. Federal security officials can declare states of exception, which permit authoritarian government.

6. Military personnel could be tried in civil courts only when the military decides it is appropriate.

Experts within Mexico, including those associated with the National Autonomous University (UNAM), have been working on models of a law that would protect citizen and human security based on U.N. concepts; such models would replace the Merida-Calderón concept of "national security" that seeks to protect State interests above a priority on public safety. These models address the causes of insecurity in communities and seek long-lasting solutions to those problems, rather than proscribe repressive actions against crime. The IACHR utilizes the following definition of "citizen security":

This group of rights includes the right to life, the right to physical integrity, the right to freedom, the right to due process and the right to the use and enjoyment of one's property, without prejudice to other rights that will be specifically examined in the body of this report.

Citizen Actions in Defense of Human Rights and for Citizen Security

The precipitous rise in violence and human rights violations and the dysfunctional nature of the Mexican justice system have led directly to the filing and acceptance of numerous cases by international courts. The Inter-American Commission on Human Rights of the Organization of American States has received numerous Mexican cases and several have been passed up to the Inter-American Court of Human Rights, which has found against the Mexican government and issued recommendations. Many of these cases pre-date the Calderón drug war but indicate the ongoing situation of impunity that forms a backdrop for the current violence.

The idea that security and human rights are a trade-off is pernicious to a rights-based society.

Mexico ratified the International Criminal Court's [ICC] Rome Statute on October 28, 2005. The ICC can accept cases if the State accused of crimes against humanity is deemed inactive, unwilling or unable to prosecute. On November 25, 2011, a case against the Calderón administration claiming crimes against humanity under the current security policy was presented with more than 23,000 signatures—a record-breaking number for the ICC. The case documents 470 instances of "crimes against humanity" including assassination, forced disappearance, torture and recruitment of minors.

The response of the Calderón government was swift, angry, and legally flawed. In a communique, the Ministry of Foreign Relations stated that "[t]he Federal Government categorically rejects that security policy can constitute an international crime." To assert that a State security policy can never constitute a crime is unprecedented and patently ridiculous. The case is awaiting a decision on acceptance from the ICC and although unlikely to be accepted formally, proponents hope to raise the issues and perhaps have the country placed under observation, as happened in a similar case involving Colombia.

A similar effort has been undertaken before the non-binding Permanent People's Tribunal (PPT), an international tribunal of conscience that formed as the successor to the Russell Tribunal. The PPT has agreed to form a Mexico chapter and receive documentation regarding the Mexican government's human rights violations.

The False Dilemma

The idea that security and human rights are a trade-off is pernicious to a rights-based society. There can be no security without human rights. The Mexican government's retort that criminals are the major violators of human rights minimizes government responsibility for ensuring a society that respects human rights and for preventing and punishing violations by state actors.

The drug war launched by the Calderón administration and supported by the U.S. Merida initiative has led to a sharp increase in human rights violations and a general climate of violence and militarization. To build respect for human rights, Mexico must reform the current security model that posits a trade-off between rights and security and work to build citizen security based on human rights and democratic participation.

6

Mexico's Drug War Has Similarities to the War on Terror

Mario Loyola

Mario Loyola is a columnist and a former foreign policy counsel to the US Senate Republican Policy Committee.

Enrique Peña Nieto's election as president of Mexico in July 2012 signals a new era in that country's fight against the drug cartels. First, the election of a candidate with close ties to a television network shows that the networks have just as much influence on national politics as the cartels. Second, it inspires hope in the Mexican people that democracy is working and that they actually have a say in governance. The latter development is essential in defeating the drug cartels. Mexico's cartel problem has a lot of similarities to the war on terror. Authorities should focus on depriving the cartels of the things they need to operate and survive—particularly the popular support of the Mexican people. Peña's victory is a hopeful sign in that ongoing war in Mexico.

Watchers of goings-on in Mexico have long worried that the drug cartels might grow powerful enough to start buying themselves whole political parties and elections. But Sunday's presidential election [on July 1, 2012], which brought the country's traditional political oligarchy back to power, shows that the cartels face a major contender for influence over national politics: television networks.

The telegenic young Enrique Peña Nieto easily won the election, bringing his Institutional Revolutionary Party (PRI) back to power for the first time in twelve years. Previously, the PRI had ruled Mexico for 71 years, establishing an upper-class oligarchy in a country that until recently was composed of a very few rich people and a huge number of desperately poor ones.

One of the campaign's dominant issues was Mr. Peña's close relationship with Televisa, the nation's leading television network, which has a dominant market share. When he was governor of the state surrounding Mexico City, he cultivated a close relationship with the network. An arrangement whereby the state provided Televisa with tens of millions of dollars in exchange for advertising and positive news coverage has become a topic of heated debate. It has further emerged that the producers at Televisa decided to raise Mr. Peña's profile through a marketing strategy that has been hugely successful for the network's soap operas: the ubiquitous *telenovelas*.

The Dashing Candidate

Vaguely evocative of a young Cary Grant, and always impeccably coiffed and polished, the dashing Mr. Peña seems less a political leader than a sex symbol: According to one poll reported in the *Wall Street Journal*, 88 percent of married Mexican women said they would cheat on their husbands with him.

People often say that he looks like a movie star. But he *is* a movie star. His image has been shaped by the country's most successful and sophisticated media producers—and they have given him a lot of airtime. The popular mantra in Mexico is that nobody believes anything politicians say, and that was a drag on Peña's candidacy. But the marketing strategy worked, and a lot of Mexicans like him. . . .

A New Era

In [Mr. Peña's] victory speech, he promised a government with a view to the future, and no return to the past. Distancing himself from the PRI's legacy of decrepit state-owned industries, corrupt administration, and protectionist economic policies, Mr. Peña has repeatedly said he would open up the oil industry to private (and foreign) investment, reform the judiciary, and liberalize the country's strict labor laws.

He will run into a lot of special interests, but the very fact that he is making unabashedly free-market proposals, and that he ran as a centrist candidate, is a clear indication of how far Mexico has come in embracing market principles. In the last two decades Mexico has gone from a stiff web of tariff barriers to nearly none, and is now one of the top countries in the world in terms of free trade. Per capita income is the third-highest in Latin America, after Argentina and Puerto Rico, and labor productivity remains well above China's. Economic growth has been sluggish in recent years, but unemployment remains low, and net illegal immigration to the U.S. has slowed to a trickle.

The fact is that nobody knows why Mexico's horrific cartel problem has not spilled over the border.

To the outside world, these gains are obscured by the horrifying violence of the drug cartels. But within Mexico, the picture is a bit more nuanced. The violence has taken 55,000 lives in six years, but it is highly concentrated along supply routes and at bottlenecks such as border towns where the cartels compete for access. Neither are the victims evenly distributed: Most are themselves members of cartels, in the wrong place at the wrong time. Most Mexicans support President Felipe Calderón's government in its policy of a fight to the end with the cartels, even if they know that the fight has led to a rise in violence. Mr. Peña has vowed to continue Calderón's fight, but the PRI has a history of cozy relations with the cartels. Still, Mexicans see little alternative to the government's policy. All of this helps explain why the drug cartels were not a major issue in this election, which focused instead on a more typical blend of economic policy and character assassination.

Mexico and the United States

In May 2009 I traveled to Mexico for an *NR* [*National Review*] feature on the drug cartels. I visited with local and federal officials in the north, middle, and south of the country, and with U.S. embassy officials in Mexico City, including an agent of the combined anti-cartel task force. I was left with one major question: Why is the violence and lawlessness of places like Ciudad Juárez not spilling over into American cities like El Paso [Texas], right across the river?

The U.S.-Mexico border is among the most porous in the world: drugs, guns, cash, and people flow back and forth unimpeded—why not also violence? You might think that American law enforcement is more effective, but it isn't, at least not when it comes to drugs on the street. Anyone in America who wants to buy illegal drugs can get them easily, usually at a reliably good price. And yet the problems that the drug trade has caused in Mexico—the shocking violence, the corruption at the highest levels of government, even the collapse of whole police forces—are nowhere to be seen in the United States. Why is that?

The consensus answer among U.S. officials—that the cartels are afraid of getting into a fight to the finish with the U.S. government—strikes me as both plausible and entirely speculative. The fact is that nobody knows why Mexico's horrific cartel problem has not spilled over the border.

One may concede that legalizing drugs in the U.S. would instantly solve the cartel problem in Mexico. However, the cartel problem in Mexico is not a byproduct of American drug policy; otherwise we'd have the same cartel problem here. It is not even a byproduct of Mexican drug policy, because in both the U.S. and Mexico drug policy has been an utter failure, and we still don't have a cartel problem here.

Mexico's inevitable victory in the war against the cartels is likely to have important things in common with the war on terror.

In that sense, Mexico's cartel problem has nothing to do with the drug war at all. Even in the teeth of a drug war, the drug trade *itself* can function nearly perfectly without all the violence, corruption, and institutional collapse that you see in Mexico. From sea to shining sea, the United States is a fantastic bazaar of illegal drugs; but we don't have to worry about whole police forces collapsing.

Look to the War on Terror

The proper way to look at Mexico's cartel problem is not through the lens of the drug war, but through that of the war on terror. After 9/11 [2001] the U.S. national-security establishment (especially the Pentagon) quickly concluded that the first line of defense against terrorism is the governance capacity of those countries where terrorists are present and can operate freely. Because global terrorist networks are transnational, the effort to counter them must also be transnational. "Partnership capacity building" became a ubiquitous mantra within the national-security establishment.

Mexico has a major problem with governance capacity. Entire police forces have collapsed. Many state and local governments cooperate with or are controlled outright by cartels. The cartels even infiltrated the president's personal bodyguard, through a combination of threats to family members and a $200,000 *monthly* retainer. With this devastating combination of bribery and threats, the cartels have gotten to scores of mayors, governors, party officials, police chiefs, municipal water authorities, you name it.

Mexico's inevitable victory in the war against the cartels is likely to have important things in common with the war on terror. First, as the Pentagon's counter-terrorism policy held, you have to deprive them of the things they need to operate and survive. In order to operate, the terrorists needed a series of practical things—the means to communicate, move money around, train, plan, recruit, and arm themselves. But in order to survive in the long run, they need popular support. Once you turn the population against them, their prospects become dim indeed.

Mexicans are now against the cartels. The problem is that they're not much more sympathetic to the government. Mexicans expect to be lied to, and are resigned to having a government that is corrupt, venal, and oligarchical.

Signs of Hope

That is both the promise and the challenge of Mexico's election. The morning after the election, the country's leading newspaper, *El Universal*, ran an editorial entitled "Winner: The Citizen." As the title suggests, the paper lauded both the manner in which the election was carried out and the high voter turnout, which it noted marked "the reactivation of a participatory citizenry." The editorial noted that these were the most watched elections in Mexican history, pointing to the role of social networks. "In sum, almost nothing is beyond public scrutiny any longer. Congratulations; that's the only way we'll accede to better levels of transparency and accountability."

The elections in Mexico have given the citizens of that country reasons for believing a bit more firmly in their democratic order—in their institutions of governance. There are also reasons to hope that the administration of Mr. Peña will further reinforce that faith. Alas, Mexico has a whole other cartel problem to contend with—one that afflicts the United

States just as badly. That problem lies in interest groups that form government cartels and seize the federal machinery to benefit themselves in the name of "justice." Under the PRI's many decades in power, the reign of interest groups became a tyranny. Now powerful forces will pull Mexico back in that direction again. Let's hope the star Mr. Peña is strong enough to resist them, because a lot is riding on his success—on both sides of the border.

7

Central American Countries Should Legalize Drugs

Jamie Dettmer

Jamie Dettmer is an independent foreign correspondent and staff writer for The Times *of London,* Sunday Telegraph, *and* Irish Sunday Tribune.

Officials in the United States are concerned with the increasing number of Central American countries calling for the decriminalizing of certain narcotics and an end to the US War on Drugs, which has largely failed in the eyes of most experts. Although there have been calls for an end to drug prohibition before, this time the sitting presidents of Guatemala, Honduras, El Salvador, and Costa Rica have joined the chorus, which has made the movement more powerful. Mexico's failed approach also lends credence to the decriminalization argument. With the Barack Obama administration cutting counter-narcotics funds to Central American countries, the momentum in the region is trending toward decriminalization.

The [Barack] Obama administration has been criticized in the past for not paying enough attention to Latin America. That's changed abruptly in recent weeks [spring 2012], with senior officials rushing to head off a rebellion that's threatening to upend the war on drugs.

The Failed War on Drugs

What has the administration spooked is the rising chorus in Latin America of politicians publicly questioning the sense of the prohibition on drugs. At this weekend's [April 14–15, 2012] Summit of the Americas in Cartagena, Colombia, several Central American leaders will outline their views on what they say is a failed war. And the Obama administration has had no choice but to allow discussion of drug legalization at the summit for the first time, although it tried to forestall it. "We are ready to discuss the issue to express our opinion on why it is not the way to address the problem," said Mike Hammer, acting U.S. assistant secretary of state for public affairs.

Calls for legalizing narcotics have been heard before in Latin America, but they previously came mostly from fringe or retired front-rank politicians. In 2009, the former presidents of Mexico, Brazil and Colombia blasted the war on drugs and demanded alternative approaches. But in recent months, for the first time, sitting presidents have been questioning the efficacy of continuing with full-scale prohibition, including the leaders of Guatemala, Honduras, El Salvador and Costa Rica.

In Central America—the region has the highest homicide rate in the world and is more deadly than Afghanistan when it comes to killings—the viewpoint that the war on drugs is producing meager results at great cost is spreading.

All of them are facing violent incursions from expansionary Mexican cartels, and are struggling to contain spiralling drug-related violence and staggering crime rates, the consequences of the region becoming a favoured transit route for cocaine and heroin processed in South America and smuggled north to consumers in the United States. Decriminalizing narcotics would deprive the region's mafias of the profits that enrich and empower them, the leaders argue.

The region's hardline drug warriors are Mexico's Felipe Calderón, who has waged a five-year-long military-based campaign against his country's powerful drug cartels that has left more than 50,000 dead, and Colombia's Juan Manuel Santos, who has been no friend to traffickers. But even they have voiced sympathy with calls for a rethink, and shocked Washington last year by raising the idea of legalizing soft drugs.

Indeed, the Mexican president argued that "if drug consumption appears impossible to stop, then the decision makers should look for more options—including market alternatives—in order to reduce the astronomical earnings of criminal organizations." Santos went further in March [2012] by initiating legislation to permit the possession of small quantities of marijuana and cocaine for personal use.

A Key Conversion

In Central America—the region has the highest homicide rate in the world and is more deadly than Afghanistan when it comes to killings—the viewpoint that the war on drugs is producing meager results at great cost is spreading. Advocates of a narcotics rethink got a boost in February when the new Guatemalan president, Otto Pérez Molina, a right-wing former army general, became a convert. The Guatemalan leader, who had promised an "iron fist" against crime when he entered office the previous month, stunned the Obama administration by announcing that the U.S. inability to cut drug consumption left his country no option but to consider legalizing narcotics.

Pérez Molina's conversion emboldened fellow Central American leaders, who declined to change their tune when U.S. Vice President Joe Biden was dispatched in early March to meet them in the Honduran capital, Tegucigalpa. The Central American rebels heard the vice-president out when he said that the U.S. wouldn't be legalizing drugs and remained determined to assist them in defeating transnational cartels with funding and intelligence sharing. But after the meeting the leaders continued to push for at least a discussion about legalization at the Summit of the Americas. All seven Central American states, plus Mexico, Colombia and the Dominican Republic, have jointly declared that "if [cutting demand] is not possible, as recent experience demonstrates, the authorities of consumer countries must explore all possible alternatives."

The U.S. Role

The Obama administration has not helped its cause by proposing, in its 2013 federal budget, to cut counter-narcotics aid to Latin America by 16 per cent. Regional leaders argue this is the reverse of what Washington should be doing. If there's to be no legalization, they say, then the U.S. and consuming countries should contribute much more to the security forces in the region and fund improvements in education and health.

> Legalization advocates argue that [Mexico's] war is an example of how, when counter-narcotics efforts are waged uncompromisingly with the full weight of the military and police, the effects can be the reverse of what's desired.

No one expects the leaders at the summit to agree to end the war on drugs. Since the meeting in Tegucigalpa, the Obama administration has lobbied regional leaders hard behind the scenes, and to some effect. A March 24 [2012] meeting called by Pérez Molina for regional leaders to discuss drug legalization ahead of the Cartagena get-together was undermined by a disappointing turnout. Although they did send senior officials, the presidents of Honduras, El Salvador and Nicaragua stayed away, amid speculation that their absence was due to U.S. pressure.

Nevertheless, former Mexican foreign minister Jorge Castañeda believes that while summits of the Americas tend to be talking shops that fail to accomplish much of significance, every now and then the multilateral get-together "actually helps to place key issues on the hemispheric table." He suspects the narcotics question could be one of them. "Whereas only a smattering of political leaders and intellectuals advocated legalization in the past, nowadays officials are coming 'out of the closet' on drugs in droves," he notes.

Legalization in Mexico

The legalization issue is likely to remain potent whatever happens in Cartagena, if for no other reason than July's Mexican presidential elections. That vote could lead to a significant toning down of Calderón's militarized war on drugs, with two of the three leading candidates who are vying to succeed the president vowing to withdraw the military from the fight. [One of these candidates, Enrique Peña Nieto, won the election.] A third candidate, Josefina Vásquez Mota, of Calderón's ruling National Action Party, is suffering in the opinion polls because of the increasing unpopularity of a drug war that seems to have no end.

Legalization advocates argue that Calderón's war is an example of how, when counter-narcotics efforts are waged uncompromisingly with the full weight of the military and police, the effects can be the reverse of what's desired. And even if such efforts showed some success, the Central American states have nothing like the firepower of the Mexican military—Costa Rica doesn't even have a standing army. Indeed, they are already outgunned: Mexico's Los Zetas cartel, infamous for its massacres and beheadings of rivals, has, according to Guatemalan officials, turned much of the country's largest department, El Petén, into a strategic stronghold.

Faced with better-armed and better-funded foes, Pérez Molina insists, "We must end the myths, the taboos, and tell people you have to discuss [legalization], discuss it, debate it."

8

US Drug Policy Needs to Change to End Mexico's Drug War

Jorge Castañeda

Jorge Castañeda is a Mexican politician, professor, author, and human rights activist. He served as foreign minister of Mexico from 2000 to 2003 and is the Global Distinguished Professor of Politics and Latin American and Caribbean Studies at New York University.

The United States will have to decriminalize or legalize drugs in order to reduce Mexico's drug cartel violence. It is the black market demand for drugs in America that has fed the Mexican cartels and has led to the horrific violence and deaths of thousands of innocent people. With the United States unwilling to provide the necessary support it would take to effectively fight the cartels—and Mexico unwilling to agree to the stipulations of such aid—the only real option is for both countries to decriminalize drugs to alleviate the power of the cartels and decrease the level of drug violence. Only if the United States changes its drug policy will Mexico be able to do the same.

American drug policy has been a central component of U.S.-Mexican relations, and of Mexican drug policy, at least since 1969, when Richard Nixon unleashed Operation Intercept at the San Ysidro—Tijuana border, inspecting every vehicle that crossed the border with the hope, not of finding any drugs, but of pressuring the government of then-President Gustavo Díaz Ordáz to expand Mexican drug enforcement. Since that time at least, the United States has followed a policy of criminalization, interdiction, and *de facto* [in fact] drug-consumption acceptance, given that American society has been reluctant to pay the price of a full-fledged attempt at zero tolerance. This has transferred a significant share of the burden of drug enforcement to the supply side of the equation, and in consequence, to the foreign policy domain.

Until very recently, an overwhelming proportion of the drugs consumed in the United States have come from abroad, and since the mid-1980s, from or through Mexico. The exception today [in 2009] begins to become marijuana, where U.S. production has probably now surpassed imports, though not by much. Drug traffickers and organized crime have reached the same conclusions as everyone else—i.e., the easiest way to enter the United States, for people, goods, services and money—is from Mexico. Thus a disproportionate concentration of U.S. drug enforcement efforts abroad have centered on Mexico. The only exception has perhaps been Plan Colombia [a plan to end armed conflict and drug trafficking in Colombia while promoting economic development] since the late nineties, but many, including this writer, believe the [Presidents Bill] Clinton–[George W.] Bush initiative was as much a counterinsurgency effort as a drug enforcement program.

The U.S. Factor

While every Mexican administration since the sixties has piously declared that it intended to intensify its drug enforcement efforts for domestic motivations—drug addiction, corruption, national security, etc—the fact is that the real reason, except possibly for the current president, Felipe Calderón [president from December 2006 to December 2012], has always been American persuasion or pressure. It's not that absent the U.S. factor Mexico would have no drug enforcement policy at all, but rather that the priority attached to it would be much lower.

This has always generated ambivalence in Mexico. From the outset of this period of U.S.-Mexican relations, there has usually been a feeling in Mexico that the United States, because of what [Secretary of State] Hillary Clinton recently called its "insatiable demand" for drugs, and because of its peculiar gun laws, has created a problem for Mexico that Mexico cannot solve. Mexico puts up the bodies, the boots on the ground, and the money, and Mexico lives with the violent consequences of an American dilemma, which Mexico believes the United States only addresses hypocritically.

It is because of American demand that Mexico is "forced" to wage a war on drugs that otherwise it would not have to fight.

This is why in general there is scant support for a tough drug enforcement stance in Mexico; most of the country's inhabitants tend to think that in this field, at least, Mexico is doing the United States' dirty work. The only way to get around this challenge has been to fabricate other explanations, which almost always are at best half-truths. This is what has taken place under President Calderón: he has provided several rationales for his crackdown—consumption in Mexico, violence, loss of state control in certain parts of the country, corruption—which, while not totally false, are at best ongoing plagues that the country has managed and lived with for decades. In the case of consumption, the rationale is simply false: Mexican drug use, according to the government's own statistics, remains remarkably low, and has barely grown over the past decade. Initially, a justification like Calderón's works well, because it casts the government's policy as homegrown and domestic-driven; but after a while the weakness of the argument begins to surface, and public opinion starts noticing a substantial gap between the magnitude of the efforts deployed and the reasons for doing so.

Mexico cannot really hope to alter its drug-enforcement approach while the United States doesn't act accordingly.

Mexico's Drug Problem Is U.S. Driven

It is worthwhile recalling that Mexico has traditionally produced marijuana and heroin, and more recently methamphetamines, but not the most attractive drug from a business perspective: cocaine. Heroin suffers from a ceiling on the number of addicts at any given time, in any given country, although it is a high-value, low-volume merchandise; marijuana is tremendously bulky given the profits it fetches, even if the universe of its consumers can and does expand; only cocaine brings together the business advantages of both drugs, without the inconveniences of either. But since coca leaf does not grow in Mexico, the country is exclusively a trans-shipper to the United States: if the latter did not exist, or did not use cocaine in any of its variations, Mexico's drug "problem" would almost vanish or, more precisely, be reduced to the traditional use of marijuana and probably the consumption of synthetic drugs by affluent teenagers in night clubs. So again, even the economics of the drug trade make Mexican policy highly U.S.-driven: it is because of American demand that Mexico is "forced" to wage a war on drugs that otherwise it would not have to fight.

All of this serves to show why current U.S. drug policy—i.e., the one in place since the sixties—would have to change in order for the Mexican stance to change. It also explains why it is virtually impossible for Mexico to follow a different policy unilaterally. When in 2005 then-President Vicente Fox attempted to modify the country's laws to decriminalize the possession of very small quantities of marijuana, heroin, and cocaine, essentially to eliminate the Mexican equivalent of the so-called Rockefeller laws [drug laws enacted in 1973 in New York State that mandate harsh prison terms for the possession or sale of relatively small amounts of drugs] and not imprison minor drug offenders, he met a ferocious resistance from the [George W.] Bush administration, which in addition to direct pressure also argued that a supposedly imminent immigration reform would be jeopardized (it was never approved anyway). Fox backed down, basically having no choice.

Mexico cannot really hope to alter its drug-enforcement approach while the United States doesn't act accordingly. We cannot legalize, decriminalize, or move to harm reduction if the United States doesn't do the same, because we would become, like Zurich in the recent past, a sanctuary for U.S. consumers of one sort or another. We cannot successfully pursue a full-fledged direct onslaught against the cartels—like Calderón has chosen to do—without both failing and paying an enormous price. And while we might be able to return to the tacit *modus vivendi* [way of living] of the past, it will not be easy, now that Mexico has asked for American support, and has at least partly received it. Washington will not willingly retract itself from the commitments and praise it has showered on Felipe Calderón if he were to draw back from his war on drugs and search for some type of accommodation (which he seems, by the way, totally opposed to doing). So where does that leave Mexican policy for the second half of the Calderón administration, and Barack Obama's first term?

Reassessing the Options

If current trends toward medical decriminalization continue, if the Webb Commission in the Senate concludes that some changes in U.S. drug laws are necessary and desirable, and if the Obama administration pursues a *de facto* harm reduction approach without explicitly stating it, there may be a way for

Mexico to extricate itself from its current, tragic predicament. Otherwise, though, there does not seem to be any accessible, affordable, and acceptable exit strategy from the current war. And Mexico will continue to pay an exorbitant cost for having plunged, with U.S. support and encouragement, into a war with no ostensible victory in sight.

As long as any Mexican president can use the army to do police work and drug-enforcement jobs, there is no reason to believe that he won't do so.

By taking on all of the cartels, all the time, throwing the Mexican military at them, and obviously not engaging with means to achieve his ends, Calderón has painted himself into a corner. The end is obviously not to eradicate drug production or trans-shipment in Mexico, but rather, to limit local processing and acreage, and to sufficiently raise the cost of using Mexican territory as an entry way to the United States to "push" the cartels away from Mexico toward other routes. The two aims require three ingredients: an effective police force for domestic law enforcement; an effective military to seal off land, sea, and air frontiers; and considerable U.S. support in training, equipment, intelligence, detection, and so forth. None of these are available at this time, nor will they be at any time soon. We will now see why.

A Failed Approach

For all practical purposes, Mexico does not have a national police force. There are roughly 2,500 municipal police corps, thirty two state police forces, and since 1999, a Federal Police (PF) actually made of two army brigades, with about 18,000 operational troops. The country also has a federal investigative police, the AFI [Agencia Federal de Investigacíon], modeled on the FBI [Federal Bureau of Investigation], which was supposed to be merged with the PF, though this ultimately proved impossible. The roughly 350,000 members of the municipal and state police departments are basically useless as law enforcement agencies, and even more so as drug enforcement entities. The last three governments ([Ernesto] Zedillo, Fox and Calderón) have known this, which is why they all tried, so far unsuccessfully, to build a national police, along the lines of Chile's *Carabineros*, or Colombia's *Policía Nacional*. Calderón founded a new police academy in 2007, but as of this writing [August 2009], and in response to direct questions posed by Human Rights Watch, for example, his government has stated that not one single combat-ready "cop" has graduated from the six-month instruction (woefully insufficient, in any case) that the academy provides. The only graduates are "intelligence analysts," which Mexico has anyway in its National Security and Intelligence Center (CISEN). As long as any Mexican president can use the army to do police work and drug-enforcement jobs, there is no reason to believe that he won't do so. And the National Police Force will remain a work in progress.

The Mexican Military

The Mexican Army is one of the most respected institutions in the country, but the government makes too much of this. Firstly, poll questions can be formulated in many different ways, and depending on the poll, the army is more or less admired. Secondly, it is liked more where it isn't stationed than where it is; and thirdly, Mexican society knows full well that the corruption scandals in the military do not just belong to the past (Zedillo's drug czar, General Gutiérrez Rebollo, was arrested in 1998 for drug trafficking). Moreover, the modern Mexican military, founded after the Revolution in the twenties, has always been held on a short leash by the civilian leadership of the country. The non-military presidents, from 1946 onward, preferred to compress—or depress—the training, equipment, professionalism and overall combat readiness of the army, largely as a way of forestalling any temptations it might have had to intervene in politics. Unlike in much of the rest of Latin America, the Mexican military is not an aristocratic corps, nor have they staged any coups or *pronunciamientos* in nearly a century. But this, then, is deliberately an army, navy, and air force unready for sophisticated, complex, multifaceted, rapid deployment operations like sealing off the southern border by air, land, and sea.

As long as criminalization, its hypocrisy, and serious discussions of the alternatives are banned from public discussion, U.S. drug policy will remain what it has been for the past forty years.

Mexico's aerospace effort began in the early nineties, with P-4 flights piloted by Mexicans but with an American advisor on board; aerostatic balloons, mini-AWACs [Airborne Warning and Control Systems], radars and swift boat pursuit groups were set up in the late nineties; more mini-AWACs were purchased from Brazil in 2001, but all of this has largely come to naught. Today, many experts believe that although according to some intelligence sources, small plane drug shipments from Colombia and Central America have already dropped significantly, Mexico, with massive U.S. support, could go further and create the equivalent of a no-fly zone in the south, where every unauthorized and unidentified aircraft would *ipso facto* [by the fact itself] be shot down without further notice. Maritime surveillance is more complex, because of the endless Mexican coastlines. Even if the navy only patrolled in the south, it would be spread across three seas: the Pacific, the Caribbean, and the Gulf of Mexico, and detecting all night time incursions, semi-submersible vessels, and other stealthy intruders would be virtually impossible. Again, the only way to do this is with the type of U.S. support that allowed Washington to cut off the South Florida routes in the mid-eighties.

Finally, the land border, given the incredible porousness of the Mexico-Guatemala border, might best be sealed off at the Isthmus of Tehuantepec, as the intelligence agency has contemplated since 2004, but again, this also would involve American cooperation, now in the Mexican hinterland, no longer just at the border.

U.S. Cooperation

Which brings us to the third issue, which we have in fact already touched upon repeatedly: U.S. cooperation. The Merida Initiative [an initiative signed into law in June 2008 which provides US money to Mexico to fight drug trafficking with investments in training, equipment, and intelligence] may have been, as both governments hailed it, a watershed in that on the one hand Washington accepted its responsibility in the drug quagmire (although it in fact has always acknowledged this since the sixties), and Mexico finally requested and received far greater sums of American aid than before (although in relative terms this is arguable: see Zedillo's receipt and return of more than sixty Vietnam-vintage "Huey" helicopters in the nineties). But this is nowhere near significant enough for the challenges outlined above.

In addition to U.S. budgetary reasons, it is insufficient because Mexico does not *want* more, given the stringent conditions which generally accompany American aid. Most importantly, and in stark contrast to Plan Colombia, where nearly one thousand U.S. personnel (openly official, or "contractual") have been operating for a decade, Mexico will not accept American "boots on the ground." This is perfectly understandable, given the two countries' history, but it is contradictory. The Pentagon and Congress will not readily provide sophisticated technology to Mexican forces if they subsequently switch sides, as the infamous "Zetas" [commandos from the Mexican army who became a drug cartel] did in the late nineties; they want to do the vetting themselves. Worse still, it costs immensely more to train Mexican forces in the United States, than to send U.S. trainers to Mexico. And lastly, in order for intelligence cooperation to function effectively, the level of trust, cooperation and real-time, on-the-ground collaboration in pursuit operations must reach levels unheard of until now. None of this is anywhere near the realm of the possible, and in all likelihood will not become feasible any time soon.

The United States Must Change Its Drug Policy

Hence the paradox U.S. drug policy has wrought. As long as criminalization, its hypocrisy, and serious discussions of the alternatives are banned from public discussion, U.S. drug policy will remain what it has been for the past forty years: a supply-side, foreign-policy, nickel-and-dime war waged beyond U.S. borders. In the case of Mexico, for a series of specific reasons, that policy, as well as domestic Mexican political considerations, have led to a war that cannot be won and should not be waged. Unless the United States is ready and able to provide much more support for Mexico, with a much longer-standing commitment, and with far greater "cultural" obstacles, than Plan Colombia. And in addition, Mexico has to let itself be helped if it wants to win the war of choice that President Calderón has embarked upon. It would have to accept conditions and terms of U.S. support that have always been anathema in the past, and that Mexican society is probably not yet ready to countenance.

There is no optimum solution to this conundrum. But the only conceivable alternative lies in a change in U.S. drug policy: not demand reduction, or supply interdiction, but decriminalization, harm reduction, adjusting laws to reality instead of uselessly attempting the opposite, and understanding that the last thing the United States needs is a fire next door.

9

Mexico's Drug War: The Battle Without Hope

Malcolm Beith

Malcolm Beith is an author who has written extensively on the Mexican drug war for such publications as Foreign Policy, Jane's Intelligence Weekly, *and* Slate. *He is the author of* The Last Narco: Inside the Hunt for El Chapo, the World's Most Wanted Drug Lord.

Despite the wave of horrific violence caused by brutal Mexican drug cartels, the United States will not push for the decriminalization of drugs as a viable option. Instead, it continues to support counter-insurgency campaigns and the militarization of Mexico's law enforcement. To date, this strategy has largely been a failure. The United States is also considering designating drug cartels as terrorists, which would at least force it to increase cooperation with Mexico. However, other Latin American leaders have called for decriminalization as the best strategy to fight the drug cartels.

The bald, middle-aged man slumps against the wall in the yard. The blood from his companion's head splatters his shirtless chest. He looks to his left, at the headless corpse lying next to him. The chainsaw continues to roar. The bald man rests his head against the wall once again. He awaits his turn.

The horrors of Mexico's drug war, which has raged since December 2006 and the start of President Felipe Calderón's administration, know no bounds. More than 50,000 people have died in drug-related violence since, and there is no sign of the bloodshed diminishing. In 2006, shortly before Calderón deployed tens of thousands of soldiers to combat the violence, a group of armed thugs rolled five heads on to the dance floor of a nightclub in central Mexico as a warning; by 2007 and 2008, beheadings had become commonplace.

In 2009, a man nicknamed El Pozolero—"the stew-maker"—was arrested and confessed to dissolving the remains of more than 300 people in vats of caustic soda for a drug kingpin. Later that year, a man working for rivals of the powerful Sinaloa cartel was found; he had been beheaded and his face had been carved off and delicately stitched on to a football. Dozens of mass graves were discovered throughout the Latin American nation last year, many of them in Tamaulipas, a north-eastern state notorious for its hazy fug of lawlessness and for the terror tactics of Los Zetas, a group of former paramilitaries who now run their own drug trafficking syndicate.

Videos of some of the atrocities have been disseminated over the internet. In the most recent one, described above, members of the Sinaloa cartel are put to death.

In Mexico, and in other countries such as Guinea-Bissau and Afghanistan, the war against drug trafficking and organised crime is a fight for social and political progress—12 years ago, Mexico became a full-fledged multiparty democracy, as the Institutional Revolutionary Party, or PRI, was ousted from 71 years of uninterrupted rule. It is also a battle to root out official corruption that for decades—in some cases, centuries—has allowed drug trafficking and other illicit activity to flourish. The violence will not end soon; even Mexican officials admit that it is unlikely the bloodshed will ebb for another six years or so, and the Mexican electorate is largely in favour of state execution for drug traffickers (polls show that about 70 per cent of Mexicans want the death penalty reinstated for narcos, as traffickers are commonly known). In July, the PRI was re-elected democratically, in spite of critics' fears that it would again turn a blind eye to organised crime.

The drug war is also a war between rival cartels fighting for control over lucrative smuggling routes while trying to maintain their structure as the authorities crack down.

The war between the Sinaloa cartel and Los Zetas—and that of the authorities against them—is a game-changer in a long, grinding process of attempting to manage drug trafficking and consumption, one that has cost US taxpayers $1 trn since it was launched in 1971 by the then president, Richard Nixon.

The Sinaloa cartel—led by Joaquín "El Chapo" Guzmán Loera, son of an opium farmer from the mountains in the north-western state of Sinaloa—has expanded in recent years to become the most powerful drug trafficking organisation in the world. Under the reign of El Chapo (meaning "shorty"), the cartel has reversed the previous business arrangement with Colombian cocaine producers, which shipped the product through the Caribbean until a law-enforcement crackdown in the 1980s made Mexico a more attractive option. The Sinaloa cartel now buys cocaine from the Colombian cartels and takes full responsibility for distribution.

The Sinaloa cartel produces its own marijuana, heroin and methamphetamine; it imports chemical precursors used to make methamphetamine from Asian nations such as India, Thailand and China. The authorities have spotted Sinaloa cartel operatives and scouts (conejos, or rabbits, in Spanish) on every continent; the Australian authorities believe the cartel is responsible for delivering as much as 500 kilogrammes of cocaine a month on to their shores.

In the spirit of globalisation, it is thought, El Chapo has bought properties in eastern Europe and throughout Latin America in an effort to launder his dirty money. In 2010 the US-based Wachovia Bank admitted to having handled $378bn for Mexican currency-exchange houses between 2004 and 2007, roughly $13bn of which was confirmed to belong to the Sinaloa cartel. (The US department of justice slapped sanctions of $160m on the bank for "wilfully failing to maintain an anti-money laundering programme".)

Last month, executives of Britain's HSBC confessed that a large portion of $7bn transferred by its Mexican subsidiaries into the bank's US operation between 2007 and 2008 probably belonged to Mexican drug cartels. "In hindsight," said David Bagley, head of compliance at HSBC, just before resigning in front of a US Senate investigative committee, "I think we all sometimes allowed a focus on what was lawful and compliant rather than what should have been best practices."

Though the Mexican drug cartels have long been considered a threat to US national security, rarely has aggressive action to counter their growth been such a popular option.

"Forget hindsight," admonished Senator Carl Levin. "Is there any way that should have been allowed to happen?" The obvious answer is no, but the Sinaloa cartel is big business and has exploited loopholes in the global banking system on unprecedented levels. Some officials warn that mafias such as the Sinaloa operation have capitalised on the global financial crisis in ways we have yet fully to understand. "The illiquidity associated with the banking crisis, the reluctance of banks to lend money to one another ... offered a golden opportunity to criminal institutions," Antonio Maria Costa, the former executive director of the United Nations Office on Drugs and Crime, said in April. "The penetration of the financial sector by criminal money has been so widespread that it would probably be more correct to say that it was not the mafia trying to penetrate the banking system, but it was the banking sector which was actively looking for capital–including criminal money . . ."

The new guard of the Mexican drug trade are Los Zetas. Originally a tight-knit paramilitary-style unit of deserters from the Mexican army special forces, they have formed independent gangs–consisting of perhaps thousands of members–that have metastasised throughout Mexico and central America in recent years, and have seized on any business opportunity that has come their way. The Zetas gangs engage in CD and DVD piracy, human trafficking and extortion. Anyone with a weapon, tattoos and a crew cut can call himself a Zeta and immediately instil a sense of terror.

Their modus operandi: enter a small town, behead a local business owner and declare the territory theirs. It was members of Los Zetas who indiscriminately massacred 72 migrants in Tamaulipas in August 2010; it was members of Los Zetas who were responsible for the killing of a US special agent in the state of San Luis Potosí in February 2011. There are worrying signs that, in the cartel's new incarnation, these gangs are consolidating. Last December, in an arrest operation spanning four north-eastern Mexican states, the security services seized nearly 1,500 radios and the same quantity of mobile phones belonging to the cartel; clearly, it had a communications network in place. In the past year, several leading Zetas have been captured or killed in far-flung parts of Mexico, evidence that they were trying to instil order in branches of the cartel operating in those parts.

Power, Corruption, and Lies

Though the Mexican drug cartels have long been considered a threat to US national security, rarely has aggressive action to counter their growth been such a popular option.

In Washington, calls to designate the cartels as terrorist groups have ratcheted up. On 13 October 2011, Ileana Ros-

Lehtinen, a Republican congresswoman for Florida and the chairman of the House foreign affairs committee, declared that "we must stop looking at the drug cartels today solely from a law-enforcement perspective and consider designating these narco-trafficking networks as foreign terrorist organisations". She added: "It seems that our sworn enemy Iran sees a potential kindred spirit in the drug cartels in Mexico."

The culture of corruption that has developed in Mexico, the failure of the rule of law in Mexico, is one of the largest contributing factors to the violence we see today.

On the same day, in written testimony to Congress entitled "Emerging Threats and Security in the Western Hemisphere: Next Steps for US Policy", the assistant secretary for terrorist financing, Daniel L Glaser, highlighted the problem of the drug cartels and mentioned El Chapo by name.

The view that there is a link between the cartels and terrorism (some expressions of this are unabashedly hyperbolic, especially the attempts to label alternative Mexican faiths a "spiritual insurgency", in line with the theories of the US Army War College's Steven Metz) has grown amid several topical developments as well as vastly improved US-Mexican co-operation in the drug war. The two countries—Mexico is the third-largest trading partner of the US—have a long, often troubled history with regard to security and intelligence-sharing.

Asa Hutchinson, the former head of the US Drug Enforcement Administration (DEA), still refuses to acknowledge that anyone besides the Mexican authorities is to blame for the failure to combat drug trafficking. "The culture of corruption that has developed in Mexico, the failure of the rule of law in Mexico, is one of the largest contributing factors to the violence we see today," he says. "Mexico has allowed itself to be a major transit and source country. They resisted US help. In

1985, Kiki Camarena, a wonderful DEA agent, was tortured and murdered in Guadalajara, and there was a massive manhunt for the perpetrators, and Mexico [took the position] that we were infringing on their sovereignty. They have resisted any US assistance ever since. The cartels have operated with impunity, and that is not the fault of the United States."

The DEA still works in Mexico, though Camarena's ghost haunts its collective memory. In 1997, Mexico's anti-drug tsar General Jesús Gutiérrez Rebollo was arrested for alleged links to the Juárez cartel. He was eventually sentenced to a total of 71 years in prison.

There have been setbacks during the outgoing Calderón administration, too. In 2008, two officials from Siedo, Mexico's special organised crime unit, were arrested for being in the pockets of the Beltrán Leyva cartel. And in December that year, an army major assigned as one of Calderón's bodyguards, Arturo González Rodríguez, was arrested and charged with feeding the cartels intelligence for $100,000 a month.

Diplomats continue to stress that US-Mexican relations, not to mention co-operation in the drug war, can survive the setbacks.

The allegations of corruption have hindered counter-drug operations: the Mexican military has had to fend off both credible accusations and propaganda disseminated by the cartels. While General Eugenio Hidalgo Eddy was stationed in Sinaloa and was in charge of local counter-drug operations, narco-mantas—banners made by drug traffickers—accusing him of protecting El Chapo were frequently found at crime scenes. Eddy insists that he fought the good fight. "Never did I make a pact! Never!" he told me, slamming his fist on his desk. "Others, I don't know," he added, quietly.

In January this year, General Manuel de Jesús Aviña was arrested and charged with ordering killings and torture and engaging in drug trafficking while stationed in the northern Chihuahua state. The Calderón administration had almost made it through its six-year term without a senior army officer being linked to traffickers. But since then, four other generals have been detained for alleged links to the cartels, including one who had served as defence attaché at the Mexican embassy in Washington, DC.

There have been allegations against US officials, too, and the ensuing questions of trust have complicated intelligence-sharing. "We're in the business of collecting information," the DEA's then chief of intelligence, Anthony Placido, told me in 2010. "The problem with trying to share it is that we have to make sure we don't kill the goose that's laying the golden eggs. We have to make sure our foreign partners are trustworthy."

Human rights abuses—children and innocent adults have been gunned down by the Mexican military and there have been allegations of torture and rape—have raised eyebrows at the state department, which has issued several scathing reports on Mexico during the Calderón administration. (The state department has also commended the country for making some much-needed improvements.) "Human rights are stupid," a former Mexican general told me.

The Next Insurgency?

Diplomats continue to stress that US-Mexican relations, not to mention co-operation in the drug war, can survive the setbacks. "At 35,000 feet, the muscle tone and the strategic direction of the US-Mexican relationship are fantastic," Mexico's ambassador to the US, Arturo Saru-khan, told me late last year. "In many ways it's like a Dickensian tale of two cities—it's the best of times and it's the worst of times. If you look at the formal diplomatic traction and relationship, it has never been better. But if you look at public perception on both sides of the border, [that] would seem to be thousands of miles from where the relationship is."

So, co-operation has continued to increase with little opposition, as has US funding for the counter-drug Mérida Initiative, which was introduced in 2008 and will eventually channel $1.6bn in anti-drug assistance to Mexico and, to a lesser extent, central America.

Through Mérida, Mexico has received Black Hawk helicopters and X-ray scanners for customs posts, as well as assistance in professionalising the police and training in the justice sector.

The question now is whether the US state department will take the step of designating the cartels as terrorist organisations.

Last year, the Pentagon began flying drones over Mexican airspace in an attempt to gather intelligence on drug trafficking suspects. There was little public dissent. Global Hawk drones have been deployed; flying as high as 60,000 feet overhead, they are able to survey 105,000 square miles in a day. A second counter-drug operations centre, where US and Mexican agencies work together in the fight against drugs, has been opened in Mexico City. US military experts regularly visit the Mexican capital to consult with the security services and offer strategic advice. The DEA has a dozen offices in the country, out of which its agents now operate in a purely advisory capacity. In January, the new CIA director general, David Petraeus, the advocate and implementor of the counter-insurgency strategy in Afghanistan and Iraq known as COIN, visited Mexico City and met with the national security adviser and the head of Mexico's spy agency, CISEN.

Calderón, who will step down in December, has repeatedly urged Washington to halt the flow of guns and cash from drug sales into Mexico (estimates of how many guns used in drug-related crimes in Mexico come from the US vary, but it is believed that Americans supply most of them). On the US side, however, there has been little in response aside from rhetoric. A new Mexican president—Enrique Peña Nieto of the PRI—was elected on 1 July, and has pledged to continue the fight against organised crime. Despite his promises, it is likely he will face suspicion from Washington because of his party's long-standing "blind-eye" attitude to organised crime.

Move On, Please

The question now is whether the US state department will take the step of designating the cartels as terrorist organisations. It has already done so with the Farc in Colombia. If Los Zetas and the Sinaloa cartel are categorised as such, the US would probably have more jurisdiction to increase co-operation with Mexico. Barack Obama's signing of the National Defence Authorisation Act on 31 December could also allow US nationals suspected of narcoterrorism to be detained indefinitely.

What is unlikely to happen, however, is any move towards drug legalisation. Advocates of the policy, who grew optimistic with Obama's election and the appointment of R Gil Kerlikowske as director of the Office of National Drug Control Policy (Kerlikowske has repeatedly said that drug consumption must be treated as a health rather than a criminal issue), continue to be marginalised.

A growing number of former Latin American leaders—and even some current ones, such as the Guatemalan president, Otto Pérez Molina—have begun to push for discussion of a fresh approach to the drug problem. Calderón, to his credit, took the risk of publicly acknowledging mounting calls for a debate on a change of counter-drug strategy; he decriminalised the possession of small quantities of almost every drug during his presidency.

American politicians are much more cautious. California, which has historically led the way on progressive laws, voted against the legalisation of marijuana in November 2010. Lacking support, the idea has been dropped from the ballot in this year's election. The conventional wisdom is that if California doesn't legalise it, no one in the United States will.

As for Mexico, the future remains unclear. Police reforms, which officials hope will instil a measure of trust in the authorities and allow state forces to maintain a semblance of security without having to resort to using the military, are slogging their way through a gridlocked congress. Peña Nieto has also proposed the creation of a national gendarmerie under civilian control. Judicial reforms, which introduced trial by jury in some Mexican states for the first time, have been enacted. However, most Mexican officials concede that it will be impossible to eradicate the drug problem entirely. Their best hope is to make Mexico so difficult for drug traffickers to navigate that they are forced to go elsewhere. Some hope indeed.

10

Mexico Drug War: Enrique Pena Nieto Could Target Small Gangs

Michael Weissenstein

Michael Weissenstein is a reporter for the Associated Press.

Mexico's new president, Enrique Pena Nieto, has signaled that he is ready to explore new strategies in his country's fight against the drug cartels that have unleashed devastating violence in the past few years. However, his reluctance to give specifics has sparked concern that he has no coherent blueprint on how to approach the drug war. Pena Nieto has assured the country that he will not turn a blind eye to drug violence. During his campaign, he pledged support for the building of a paramilitary police force, known as a National Gendarmerie; proposed an increase in security spending; and favored consolidating Mexico's local police forces.

Mexico's next president has boldly promised to halve the number of kidnappings and murders during his six-year term by moving law enforcement away from showy drug busts and focusing on protecting ordinary citizens from gangs.

Yet Enrique Pena Nieto said remarkably little specific about his anti-crime strategy during the three-month campaign that ended with his still-contested victory in Sunday's election.

That ambiguity has fed fears at home and abroad that Pena Nieto might look the other way if cartels smuggle drugs northward without creating violence in Mexico. Many analysts wonder if Pena Nieto is holding back politically sensitive details of his plans, or simply doesn't know yet how he'll prosecute the next stage of Mexico's drug war.

Some hints are starting to seep out. A close acquaintance, U.S. Rep. Henry Cuellar of Texas, told The Associated Press that the president-elect has discussed a new offensive against the smaller, local gangs that have cropped up in many Mexican states and earn money through kidnapping and extortion in addition to drug dealing.

President Felipe Calderon's 5 1/2-year war against the big cartels has been criticized by some for fracturing control of territory and smuggling routes, spawning smaller gangs like La Linea in Chihuahua state and La Barredora in the city of Acapulco that view ordinary citizens as their primary source of illicit income.

"In Mexico you have the drug cartels and then you've got regional gangs that are taking advantage of what's happening there," Cuellar said. "That is what he means by reducing the violence: Go after those folks who are actually hurting, assaulting and kidnapping people."

Analysts have said any new focus necessarily means fewer of Mexico's limited resources would go to fighting the biggest smugglers of drugs to the U.S.

But Cuellar, who has met with Pena Nieto several times in the U.S. and Mexico, stressed that the man who will become president Dec. 1 insists he will still target larger organizations such as the Zetas and Sinaloa cartels, the rival groups that have become Mexico's dominant criminal organizations.

"He's told me he's going to go after everybody," Cuellar said. "He said, 'It's the drug cartels and the gangs, and I'm going to reduce the violence.'"

Since Sunday's vote, Pena Nieto has repeatedly promised to continue Calderon's confrontation with cartels, sending messages to both Mexican and U.S. audiences that his new approach will not mean quiet accords with drug gangs in exchange for a reduction in violence that has killed more than 47,500 people since late 2006.

Many voters said . . . that they were voting for the PRI in part because they believed its return to power would bring back those backroom deals and reduce violence.

"We will wage an effective fight against the capos, against the heads of the cartels, but clearly also with a rethinking that will allow a lowering of violence," Pena Nieto told a small group of reporters Monday. "There will be no truce, no pact with organized crime."

Pena Nieto's Institutional Revolutionary Party, or PRI, ran Mexico for 71 unbroken years of autocratic rule that ended in 2000, and it was accused of systemic corruption that included payoffs from drug lords in exchange for protection.

Despite Pena Nieto's firm disavowals, many voters said Sunday that they were voting for the PRI in part because they believed its return to power would bring back those backroom deals and reduce violence.

Among those skeptical about a return of the PRI has been U.S. Sen. John McCain of Arizona, who congratulated Pena Nieto on Twitter, followed by: "will be interesting to see how he approaches drug trafficking & other issues of mutual concern."

A day later, Pena Nieto thanked McCain and tweeted his response: "In the struggle against drug trafficking, Mexico's undeniable obligation, we will look for immediate results."

Pena Nieto has signaled that he is open to consideration of new approaches to the drug war, saying during the campaign and again this week that he favors a debate on legalization of drugs, even though he opposes the idea personally.

But so far, Pena Nieto's few concrete proposals point more toward continuity than change.

Since his victory, Pena Nieto has repeated a campaign pledge to build a 40,000-member paramilitary police force that would be dispatched to areas most in the grip of organized crime.

The idea for such a force appears at least partly aimed at assuaging critics of Calderon's overwhelming dependence on Mexican soldiers and marines to confront drug cartels. Rights groups and policing experts say that approach brought human rights violations, an overemphasis on force and delays in building capable civilian police forces.

Pena Nieto's new gendarmes, however, would be largely recruited from the ranks of the armed forces, raising questions about whether the proposal is simply a repackaging of Calderon's use of the military.

The president-elect offered one new detail about the proposed National Gendarmerie on Monday, writing in *The New York Times* that the force would be deployed specifically to rural areas.

The similarity of Pena Nieto's publicly announced plans to those of his predecessor has fed doubts.

Alejandro Hope, a security analyst and former official in Mexico's CISEN intelligence agency, described the gendarmerie plan as "half-baked." He said it could weaken the armed forces by pulling away experienced troops, and he warned against moving security resources out of violent urban areas where they are badly needed, particularly in deeply troubled border states like Coahuila and Tamaulipas.

"Who's going to be patrolling the streets of Nuevo Laredo, Torreon?" Hope said. "I think they haven't thought through their position."

Pena Nieto also says he wants to increase security spending and nearly double the ranks of the federal police by 35,000 officers, continuing Calderon's strategy of bolstering the national force and using it in places where local law enforcement is weak or corrupt.

And he wants to consolidate Mexico's thousands of notoriously ineffective local police departments with the 31 state forces, another idea proposed but only partially completed under Calderon.

The similarity of Pena Nieto's publicly announced plans to those of his predecessor has fed doubts.

"I'm more and more convinced that they don't really have a blueprint," said Eric Olson, associate director of the Mexico Institute at the Woodrow Wilson International Center for Scholars in Washington.

Pena Nieto's record as governor of the State of Mexico, which adjoins Mexico City, also points to the likelihood of continuity in the national drug war. His term saw aggressive policing against organized crime, but unremarkable results in the numbers of violent crimes.

In a move widely seen as a gesture to reassure the U.S. of his commitment to the war on drugs, Pena Nieto has hired the respected former head of Colombia's national police, retired Gen. Oscar Naranjo, to be an outside adviser to the security Cabinet that has yet to be named.

Naranjo has offered no hints of any proposals he has for Mexico, however, and that has brought skepticism about whether he will be able to influence decisions from outside the Cabinet and the military chain of command.

"Naranjo is not going to play any significant role whatsoever. He's a PR stunt," Hope said. "He's going to write a couple of papers and give a couple of conferences."

One brake on Pena Nieto's power will be his unexpected small margin of victory, winning roughly 38 percent of the presidential vote for a less than seven point lead over leftist Andres Manuel Lopez Obrador. Also, the PRI won't have a majority in either house of Congress.

A similar situation hampered Calderon's ability to push through Congress his proposed structural reforms for Mexican law enforcement. But some experts think Pena Nieto's political skills will allow him to get legal changes.

"He has skills that Calderon didn't. He has first-rate operators and he's a first-rate political operator," said Luis Rubio, president of the Center for Development Research, an independent think tank.

11

The Merida Initiative Is Misguided and Needs to Be Recalibrated

Manuel Pérez-Rocha

Manuel Pérez-Rocha is an associate fellow at the Institute for Policy Studies, where he coordinates the Networking for Justice on Global Investment project. Prior to that he directed the NAFTA [North American Free Trade Agreement] Plus and the SPP [Security and Prosperity Partnership of North America] Advocacy project, also at the Institute of Policy Studies.

In 2008, the United States approved a $400 million aid package for Mexico to fight the drug cartels. Known as the Merida Initiative, the package is poorly conceived because it focuses too much on military hardware and not enough on judicial reform, fighting corruption, and addressing the root causes of drug trafficking in Mexico. The United States should also be supporting economic, social, and land reforms that facilitate legal industries and alleviate poverty and social instability in Mexico. One good sign is that the US government has taken responsibility for its part in the Mexican drug war, and it should build on that step by initiating a real debate on drug policy, US drug laws, and the Security and Prosperity Partnership (SPP) of North America—an effort to increase cooperation between the United States, Mexico, and Canada that unfairly favors US corporate and security interests at the expense of social stability in Mexico.

Manuel Pérez-Rocha, "The Failed War on Drugs in Mexico," Heinrich Böll Foundation, March 25, 2009.

The United States has released the first $296 million dollars of a $400 million counter-drug assistance package approved in June 2008 by the US Congress for Mexico. This aid package, termed the Merida Initiative and also referred to by many civil society organisations as "Plan Mexico" (in reference to similarities with the Plan Colombia [a similar plan designed to combat drug trafficking in Colombia]), has become one of the key elements in the joint US-Mexico anti-drug strategy. The $400 million dollars are part of the first year of US security assistance for Mexico and Central America; the Central American countries, the Dominican Republic and Haiti, received $65 million from the US for this time period. President [George W.] Bush originally proposed a three-year $1.4 billion dollar aid package for Mexico based on his March 2007 visit with Mexican President Felipe Calderon in Merida, Mexico.

Although the recognition by the United States of its shared responsibility for drug trafficking and drug related violence is encouraging, the aid package and strategy itself are misguided and ill conceived because they are based on the imperatives of the Security and Prosperity Partnership of North America. The Merida Initiative concentrates too much money on hardware, particularly military hardware and not enough on the root causes of drug trafficking and the related problems of violence and corruption. Less than a quarter of the assistance will be spent on judicial reform, institution-building and other activities aimed at strengthening the rule of law and combating corruption in Mexico.

At the same time, what is glaringly absent are any additional commitments from the US for enhanced domestic efforts to curb demand for drugs and to address arms trafficking issues. Drug-related violence resulted in more than 5,700 killings in 2008 alone and more than 10,000 thousand in the present administration. . . . Human rights organisations in Mexico and the United States fear that the military hardware may be used by the Mexican military as part of its repression of social discontent, dissidence and protest given the steep rise of economic hardship during Calderon's administration

A Violent and Failed Crackdown

During the two years of Felipe Calderon's presidency Mexico has experienced unprecedented levels of drug-related violence. As the drug trafficking organisations battle for turf, local drug markets and routes into the United States, the Mexican government's strategy has shown itself to be incompetent, misguided and subordinated to the imperatives of the United States' war on terror.

The growing perception in Mexico that the government has failed in its endeavour to tackle the drug cartels has been exacerbated by attacks to the civilian population like the one on September 15, 2008 in Morelos, Michoacan, which left eighty people dead. A recent *Washington Post* editorial [September 10, 2008] indicated that "more Mexican soldiers and police officers have died fighting the country's drug gangs in the past two years than the number of U.S. and NATO [North Atlantic Treaty Organization] troops killed battling the Taliban." Of the thousands of people that died in 2008 in drug-related violence, at least 500 were police and soldiers.

The SPP is mostly about bringing prosperity to large corporations who want to remove all obstacles to unfettered investment and security for the United States.

The Mexican government has adopted several strategies to address public security and organised crime in the country. However, to tackle this problem in the coming years it is necessary to understand how the Mexican government's war on drugs and the US security assistance package to Mexico fit within the logic of the framework of the much criticised Security and Prosperity Partnership (SPP) of North America that has tied Mexico and Canada to the imperatives of George W. Bush's war on terror. It is too soon to discern the new course that President Barack Obama may give to the United States' binational relationship with Mexico and if the SPP is to continue.

The Exclusive Security and Prosperity Partnership of North America

The Security and Prosperity Partnership of North America (SPP) was launched in March of 2005, as a "trilateral effort to increase security and enhance prosperity among the United States, Canada and Mexico through greater co-operation and information sharing". This trilateral initiative was announced as "our security (Canada, Mexico and the U.S.) and our economic prosperity being mutually reinforcing". Therefore, according to official definitions the SPP "provides the framework to ensure that North America is the safest and best place to live and do business. It includes ambitious security and prosperity programs to keep our borders closed to terrorism yet open to trade" and it "builds upon, but is separate from, our long-standing trade and economic relationships. It energises other aspects of our co-operative relations, such as the protection of our environment, our food supply, and our public health."

The SPP consists of a Security Agenda that includes the creation of a perimeter of enhanced security in the North American region, namely against "external threats" and "internal threats" within the region, as well as increasing the "efficiency of safe and low risk transit" through the shared borders; and a Prosperity Agenda: for the promotion of further deregulation in trade and investment to boost "competitiveness". This agenda is also known by civil society organisations as the "NAFTA Plus" [NAFTA stands for North American Free Trade Agreement] and includes building infrastructure projects, the further removal of trade tariffs and rules of origin, reducing the transaction costs of trade, and promoting regulatory harmonisation.

As the critics of a wide array of civil society organisations in the three countries of the North American region state, the SPP is mostly about bringing prosperity to large corporations who want to remove all obstacles to unfettered investment and security for the United States by means of drawing up changes to Canadian and Mexican regulations and procedures so they will be in sync with Washington's security agenda. The SPP is defined as the "agreement in which the executives of the three countries along with the CEOs of great transnationals and the military industry attempt to impose on our peoples through a transnational, oligarchic and militarist project, another mechanism for the geo-economic and geo-strategic expansion of the United States not only at a regional but also at hemispheric and global levels". (Some of the main critics in Mexico include the Mexican Action Network on Free Trade.). . .

The dependency on the military has been at the expense of adopting much needed reforms to Mexico's police and judicial institutions.

A Lack of Democratic Oversight

The main concerns in terms of process include the lack of democratic oversight, the exclusion of civil society and the media and in contrast the participation of large corporations (through the ad-hoc North American Competitiveness Council) as the only "stakeholders". These politics of exclusion have contributed to the polarisation of the US public, adding fuel to anti-immigrant sentiment in the country and causing a reaction against Mexican migrants. . . . In terms of content, the SPP aims to continue the economic and financial deregulation for trade and investment; contribute to advancing the agenda for securing energy sources for the United States (oil, gas, water); create multifunctional transport corridors without environmental considerations; and contribute to ongoing agreements on regulatory convergence to US standards. In relation to security the purpose is to scale up measures to secure the U.S. borders as well as an intensification of regional militarisation including the extraterritorial presence and influence of the US military.

The Merida Initiative, although not a direct result of the SPP trilateral bureaucratic apparatus of 20 working groups, is a bi-national product of the same logic designed by the United States, and it contributes to enhance the incorporation of the Mexican military in counter-drug operations. It has been during the presidencies of Vicente Fox (2000–2006) and Felipe Calderón (2006 to date) [end of 2012], both from the conservative National Action Party (PAN), that a "combination of economic-business and military-police strategies have opened up according to two interlinked designs of the White House: the SPP and the Merida Initiative". Critics of the SPP explain that the trinational agenda for "deep integration" means the looting of natural resources (gas, oil, minerals, water, and biodiversity) in tandem with a labour apartheid with a sharp exclusion of the population and of congresses. The SPP is also the wider framework by which the United States has guaranteed that its two neighbours to the North and South subordinate and adopt measures, like the Merida Initiative, to guarantee its security priorities and extend its security perimeter.

The Failed War on Drugs in Mexico

On its part, the Mexican federal government's strategy to combat organised crime must be seen in relation to its need to gain legitimacy after the much questioned 2006 electoral process and the growing political, economic and social fragility in the country. This is particularly the case in the expanded use of the Mexican military in counter-drug operations throughout the country, which should correspond to the civilian police forces. The dependency on the military has been at the expense of adopting much needed reforms to Mexico's police and judicial institutions to have effective police and judiciaries who are free from corruption and who are able to identify, prosecute and punish drug traffickers.

The main component of the Mexican government's strategy to counter drug trafficking has been the massive deployment of soldiers and the federal police in 14 states in the country; it is estimated that over 35,000 soldiers have been involved in these operations. In spite of the government's efforts, drug trafficking organisations have expanded their reach in Mexico—80 Mexican municipalities are considered to be dominated by the drug cartels—and some groups have expanded their operations beyond drug trafficking to also include extortion, kidnapping and pirated goods. Drug-related violence in Mexico has also expanded at alarming rates. During 2008 the number of drug-related killings jumped to approximately 5,700, almost doubling 2007 figures. Staggeringly, 400 killings have occurred during the first 25 days of 2009.

Four Hundred Killings in the First Twenty-Five Days of 2009

The Mexican government has stated that the increase in violence in Mexico is a sign of the success of their counter-drug strategy as traffickers compete for fewer routes to traffic drugs into the United States. However, other factors are also at play such as the control over the leadership of organisations—particularly due to the detention of key capos [drug lords] in recent years—, efforts by rivals to take advantage of this leadership void in some organisations to take over territories or routes, as well as the Institutional Revolutionary Party's (PRI) loss of control over the federal, state and local government as many argue that previously the PRI "served as a referee for the drug 'cartels', regulating, controlling, and containing the drug trade, while also protecting drug trafficking groups and mediating conflicts between them."

Given the different forms of power vacuum among the cartels, violence has been adopted as the only way for traffickers to settle scores, enforce deals with customers and intimidate law enforcement agencies. In this climate of escalated violence, innocent civilians are increasingly becoming caught in the crossfire, taken as hostages or, as in the case of the attack on Morelia, the target of terrorist intimidation. Another effect of this escalation is that "the most efficient trafficking networks survive. Not only do they survive, but they thrive because law enforcement has destroyed the competition for them by picking off unfit traffickers and letting the most evolved ones take over lucrative trafficking space".

Mexican Drug Cartels

In this sense, equally concerning is the fact that the Mexican drug cartels have been increasing their presence in the United States, Central America and even South America, indicating that they seek to diversify their operations to other continents.

The Merida Initiative . . . is deficient, misdirected and one-sided.

The failure to develop a comprehensive long-term strategy to address organised crime and drug trafficking in Mexico suggests that the government has not taken into account "the clear lesson of nearly two decades of efforts to confront powerful trafficking organisations: quick fix solutions divert attention and resources from the long-term reforms in the police and justice sector that are needed to deal effectively with the inter-related problems of illicit drugs, crime and violence. More military involvement in the 'drug war' has increased corruption within the institution, generated human rights violations and failed to make a dent in the narcotics trade."

The Merida Initiative and Its Shortcomings

Mexico's efforts to combat drug trafficking and address its security crisis cannot be seen in isolation from US counter-drug policies and the framework of US security policy towards the region under the SSP. The Merida Initiative—a security assistance package presented by the [George W.] Bush Administration in October 2007 for three years of funding to combat drug trafficking, organised crime and other security threats in Mexico, Central America, Haiti and the Dominican Republic—is a key aspect of this strategy.

The participation of the Mexican Army in public security tasks is of great concern given their human rights record and their lack of accountability to civilian institutions.

The Merida Initiative, however, is deficient, misdirected and one-sided. The first year of the aid package concentrates its funding on helicopters, planes and other equipment and technology, while placing little emphasis on supporting reforms to Mexico's judiciary and civilian public security institutions. Although the Calderon's government has been right in calling on the US to do more domestically to provide additional funding for drug rehabilitation and prevention programs, exercise a tighter control over raw materials for drugs that arrive from Asia via California, increase control over money laundering and provide more oversight over the loose regulations that govern gun sales which facilitate their trafficking into Mexico—the Merida Initiative has not resulted in any increased commitments from the US government on these issues and has been accepted by the Mexican government as such.

The War on Drugs and Human Rights

Due to the efforts of some human rights organisations, the Merida Initiative includes withholding 15% of police and military funding until the State Department reports to the US Congress on the efforts made in Mexico to improve police transparency and accountability and ensure investigations into human rights abuses committed by federal policy and members of the military. The use of the military in counter-drug operations, as supported in the Merida Initiative, is an important concern for human rights organisations in Mexico who have already documented multiple human rights abuses in these operations. Several international and regional human rights mechanisms have repeatedly expressed their concern on the participation of the Mexican military in public security tasks.

Since the 1980s, subsequent presidents of Mexico have increasingly incorporated the armed forces in drug control efforts and, more recently, in public security operations by which the Mexican Army has assumed the role of the police corps, combating drug trafficking, fighting against terrorism and in the contention of social and insurgent movements. Moreover, the Defence Ministry's (SEDENA) Sectorial Program for National Defence (Programa Sectorial de Defensa Nacional) establishes a role for the Army in the fight against drug trafficking and organised crime until at least the end of Calderon's government in 2012.

The Mexican Army and Public Security

The participation of the Mexican Army in public security tasks is of great concern given their human rights record and their lack of accountability to civilian institutions. Since 2000, the National Human Rights Commission (CNDH) has received 2,966 complaints against the military of which 983 occurred in the context of the military-dominated counter-drug operations launched by Calderon in December 2006. In the same period (2000–2008) the military have committed 6,874 violations to civil guarantees. In 2008 alone, the CNDH issued 14 recommendations to SEDENA for grave human rights violations committed by members of the military; the majority of these abuses took place during counter-drug operations in the states of Tamaulipas, Michoacán, Sonora and Sinaloa. These violations included the death of seven civilians, including one minor, torture, arbitrary detention, violations to juridical security and being held incommunicado.

According to the CNDH, the military presence in public security actions covers the country from South to North, the inclusion of the military in public security bodies is increasing and their intervention in the prevention of crime and to combat delinquency is an undeniable fact, not withstanding that the federal government itself has recognised that it is necessary to withdraw the military gradually from these tasks; it is a situation that gravely endangers the system of public liberties and human rights in the country.

International co-operation for combating drug trafficking in Mexico is necessary but it should be focused on structural reforms to the police and judicial systems and include full observance of human rights and civil society participation.

An Escalation of the Criminalisation

Concerns regarding military abuses fit within the general context of human rights abuses in Mexico, the failure to comply with the recommendations made by international, regional and national human rights bodies, and several legal reforms that represent a setback for the respect for human rights. Examples of this situation include the alarming escalation of the criminalisation of dissidence and social protests, like those against the expropriation processes of communal and social goods, or commons, and modifications to the Article 27 of the Constitution by which foreign companies could engage in the exploitation of non renewable energy. In 2007 alone, the National Network of Human Rights Organizations, "All Rights for All" registered 60 cases of the criminalisation of social protest in 17 states of the country; 32 cases refer to human rights violations in the framework of economic development projects (roads, dams, mining, etc.) and 20 cases are specific to social protests linked to the demands for economic, social, cultural and environmental rights.

Moreover, the deregulation and profit-maximisation nature of the "prosperity" components of the SPP will only exacerbate conflicts of this nature in Mexico. The push for greater access for transnational corporations to land and natural resources and the lack of consultation with the local population for "development" projects is a pattern that will continue under the present regime. There are several examples of recurrent violations of economic, social and cultural rights of the population to give way to private projects where the military presence is imminent. Equipping the military for the struggle against drug trafficking is increasingly seen in Mexico as pretext within the growing tendency to label protesters and social activists as delinquents. The criminalisation of social protest and the growing militarisation of civilian life so that it is the military that confronts protests and social discontent are marking a very dangerous path for the future of Mexico.

Reforming the Merida Initiative

International co-operation for combating drug trafficking in Mexico is necessary but it should be focused on structural reforms to the police and judicial systems and include full observance of human rights and civil society participation. Therefore, future years of the Merida Initiative should not include support for the military, nor additional equipment and hardware, but rather focus on co-operation mechanisms that strengthen Mexico's efforts to increase the accountability and professionalisation of its law enforcement institutions, combat corruption and assist in the implementation of reforms to Mexico's judicial institutions.

Likewise, structural economic changes that help Mexicans maintain their livelihoods through licit activities are urgent. Deregulation policies and free trade agreements have given a hand to abusive processes for the appropriation and privatisation of communal lands and territories causing massive displacement and unemployment, which provoke social unrest that is unduly met by the government with military-dominant forces. Also, massive economic and social dislocation serves the narcoeconomy.

On the part of the United States, although President Obama has expressed support for the Merida Initiative, he has also stated that more attention needs to be given in the US to issues of domestic drug consumption and several members of Congress are also interested in beginning a debate on US drug policy. Likewise, there are initiatives in Congress that, if passed, would address some deficiencies in US gun laws and enhance enforcement efforts for illicit gun sales. As the new administration and Congress move forward we will be able to see whether future US-Mexico anti-drug co-operation may be shifting in the right direction.

Moreover, the undemocratic and corporate-led Security and Prosperity Partnership of North America (SPP) should be stopped because it excludes Congressional oversight, lacks any consultation with civil society, leads to further deregulation that benefits only corporations and has increased militarisation and violation of civil liberties.

Organizations to Contact

The editors have compiled the following list of organizations concerned with the issues debated in this book. The descriptions are derived from materials provided by the organizations. All have publications or information available for interested readers. The list was compiled on the date of publication of the present volume; names, addresses, phone and fax numbers, and e-mail and Internet addresses may change. Be aware that many organizations take several weeks or longer to respond to inquiries, so allow as much time as possible.

Bureau of Alcohol, Tobacco, Firearms and Explosives (ATF)
99 New York Ave. NE, Room 5S 144, Washington, DC   20226
(800) 800-3855
website: www.atf.gov

The Bureau of Alcohol, Tobacco, Firearms and Explosives describes itself as "a unique law enforcement agency in the United States Department of Justice that protects our communities from violent criminals, criminal organizations, the illegal use and trafficking of firearms, the illegal use and storage of explosives, acts of arson and bombings, acts of terrorism, and the illegal diversion of alcohol and tobacco products." Through its office in Mexico, the ATF helps to coordinate law enforcement efforts against violent criminal gangs that traffic illegal weapons across the US-Mexico border. The ATF website offers access to press releases, speeches, and testimony of ATF officials, and a range of publications on firearms, explosives, and other topics of interest.

Central Intelligence Agency (CIA)
Office of Public Affairs, Washington, DC   20505
(703) 482-0623 • fax: (703) 482-1739
website: www.cia.gov

Established in 1947, the Central Intelligence Agency is the civilian intelligence agency of the US government. It is responsible for gathering intelligence on foreign governments and terrorist organizations and provides national security assessments to US policymakers. The CIA's intelligence-gathering activities range from assessing emerging and existing threats to the US government, monitoring and analyzing correspondence and Internet communications, implementing tactical operations in foreign countries, developing and managing intelligence assets, launching counterterrorism efforts, to dealing with threats to the US computer systems. A major role of the CIA is to find information on terrorist threats to the United States, including ones posed by foreign drug cartels. The CIA website offers a featured story archive, recent press releases and statements, speeches and testimony by CIA officials, and a page for students to learn about CIA initiatives.

Council on Foreign Relations (CFR)
1777 F St. NW, Washington, DC   20006
(202) 509-8400 • fax: (202) 509-8490
website: www.cfr.org

The Council on Foreign Relations is an independent, non-profit membership organization and think tank that focuses on providing analysis and commentary on US foreign policy for government officials, business owners, journalists, educators, activists, and civic leaders. CFR features a studies program that generates independent research, policy briefs, and analysis and holds roundtable discussions to bring together experts, senior government officials, media pundits and journalists, and policymakers to debate issues and come up with concrete policy recommendations and innovative solutions to foreign policy issues. CFR publishes *Foreign Affairs*, a journal on international affairs and foreign policy, as well as a number of policy briefs, analyses, backgrounders, blogs, and expert briefs that can be accessed on the CFR website.

Drug Policy Alliance (DPA)
131 W 33rd St., 15th Floor, New York, NY   10001
(212) 613-8020 • fax: (212) 613-8021
e-mail: nyc@drugpolicy.org
website: www.drugpolicy.org

The Drug Policy Alliance is one of the leading organizations in the United States promoting alternative drug policy. The DPA advocates policies that reduce the harms of both drug misuse and drug prohibition, and work to ensure that drug policies no longer arrest, incarcerate, disenfranchise, and otherwise harm millions of nonviolent people. The DPA seeks to influence the legislative process by opposing draconian and harmful initiatives and promoting sensible drug policy reforms. The group has been active in California's Propositions 5 and 36, reforming the Rockefeller Drug Laws in New York, and the Safety First movement in New Jersey. The DPA has published several in-depth reports on various drugs and their effects on communities, drug policy, and legislative initiatives by experts in the field, which are available on its website.

National Council of La Raza (NCLR)

Raul Yzaguirre Bldg., 1126 16th St. NW, Suite 600
Washington, DC   20036
(202) 785-1670 • fax: (202) 776-1792
e-mail: comments@nclr.org
website: www.nclr.org

The National Council of La Raza is a nonprofit organization that advocates for better employment and economic opportunities for the Latino community. It also works to reduce poverty and eliminate housing and employment discrimination. NCLR is quite active in lobbying for immigration reform, developing and implementing health education programs, and building valuable job skills and educational opportunities for Hispanic youth. Research is also a key component of NCLR's mission, and on their website you can find research studies, fact sheets, in-depth issue analysis, and expert testimony. The website also features a blog, which offers the latest news on NCLR events and initiatives as well as the latest news that impacts the Latino community.

StoptheDrugWar.org

PO Box 18402, Washington, DC   20036
(202) 293-8340 • fax: (202) 293-8344
website: stopthedrugwar.org

StoptheDrugWar.org was founded in 1993 as the Drug Reform Coordination Network (DRCN), one of the first online organizations to take on drug policy and call for significant reforms to drug laws. StoptheDrugWar.org remains at the forefront of drug decriminalization efforts, describing its mission as working for "an end to drug prohibition worldwide and an end to the 'drug war' in its current form." To this end, it coordinates grassroots coalitions working toward the same goal; publishes a range of information on the failure of the drug war and the potential of decriminalization policies; and advocates for workable drug decriminalization policies. The Stop theDrugWar.org website provides access to the *Drug War Chronicle*, a weekly newsletter, and a blog that offers discussion of recent news, events, legislation, and initiatives.

US Customs and Border Protection (CBP)

1300 Pennsylvania Ave. NW, Washington, DC   20229
(877) CBP-5511
website: www.cbp.gov

A part of the US Department of Homeland Security (DHS), US Customs and Border Protection is the federal agency responsible for keeping terrorists and illegal weapons out of the United States. CBP trains and monitors US border patrol agents; enforces US border laws, regulations, and policies; secures US borders; and protects trade from terrorist attack, corruption, and theft. One of its most challenging responsibilities is confronting the myriad of problems posed by violent drug cartels and the lucrative drug trade between Mexico and the United States. The CBP website features a range of information on the department and its activities: videos, a photo gallery, fact sheets, statistics, and other resources.

US Department of Homeland Security (DHS)

12th & C St. SW, Washington, DC   20024
(202) 282-8000
website: www.dhs.gov

The Department of Homeland Security is tasked with protecting the United States from terrorist attacks and other threats. Established after the terrorist attacks of September 11, 2001, the DHS aims to reduce the vulnerability of US infrastructure and installations, government officials, and major events to attacks of any kind; enforce and administer immigration laws to better control who is traveling in and out of the country; coordinate and administer the national response to terrorist attacks and be a key player in recovery and rebuilding efforts; and to safeguard and secure cyberspace by assessing cyber threats and coordinating a counterattack. The DHS oversees US Custom and Border Protection (CBP), which monitors and protects the US border with Mexico. The DHS website allows access to a number of informative resources, including fact sheets, breaking news, press releases, speeches and testimony of DHS officials, video, and other publications on topics of interest.

US Department of State

2201 C St. NW, Washington, DC   20520
(202) 647-4000
website: www.state.gov

The US Department of State is the federal agency responsible for formulating, implementing, and assessing US foreign policy. The State Department also assists US citizens living or traveling abroad; promotes and protects US business interests all over the world; and supports the activities of other US federal agencies in foreign countries. The State Department is very active in enacting diplomatic efforts and informing the US Congress, the president, and the public about the political, economic, and social events. It also oversees the Bureau of Counterterrorism (CT), which is focused on developing coordinated strategies to defeat terrorists abroad and in advancing the counterterrorism objectives of the United States. The State Department website features a wealth of information on current policies, upcoming events, daily schedules of top officials, and updates from various countries. It also has video, congressional testimony, speech transcripts, background notes, human rights reports, and strategy reviews.

US Drug Enforcement Administration (DEA)

Mailstop: AES, 8701 Morrissette Dr., Springfield, VA   22152
(202) 307-1000
website: www.dea.gov

The US Drug Enforcement Administration is a department of the US Department of Justice that is focused on enforcing the nation's drug laws and reducing the amount of illegal drugs available to consumers in the United States. The DEA investigates and prosecutes drug gangs and smugglers; collaborates with legislators and policymakers to formulate an effective and comprehensive drug policy; and coordinates with other countries and international organizations to confront international drug smuggling. The DEA is responsible for enforcing federal drug laws and determining the federal approach to the treatment of state drug policies. The DEA publishes *Dateline DEA*, a biweekly electronic newsletter that provides updates on recent campaigns and new policies, as well as *Speaking Out Against Drug Legalization*.

Bibliography

Books

Ricardo C. Ainslie *The Fight to Save Juárez: Life in the Heart of Mexico's Drug War.* Austin, TX: University of Texas Press, 2013.

Malcolm Beith *The Last Narco: Inside the Hunt for El Chapo, the World's Most Wanted Drug Lord.* New York: Grove Press, 2010.

Charles Bowden *Murder City: Ciudad Juárez and the Global Economy's New Killing Fields.* New York: Nation Books, 2010.

Howard Campbell *Drug War Zone: Frontline Dispatches from the Streets of El Paso and Juárez.* Austin, TX: University of Texas Press, 2009.

Isaac Campos *Home Grown: Marijuana and the Origins of Mexico's War on Drugs.* Chapel Hill, NC: University of North Carolina Press, 2012.

George W. Grayson and Samuel Logan *The Executioner's Men: Los Zetas, Rogue Soldiers, Criminal Entrepreneurs, and the Shadow State They Created.* New Brunswick, NJ: Transaction Publishers, 2012.

Ioan Grillo *El Narco: Inside Mexico's Criminal Insurgency.* New York: Bloomsbury Press, 2011.

Paul Rexton Kan   *Cartels at War: Mexico's Drug-Fueled Violence and the Threat to US National Security*. Washington, DC: Potomac Books, 2012.

Jerry Langton   *Gangland: The Rise of the Mexican Drug Cartels from El Paso to Vancouver*. Mississauga, Ontario, Canada: J. Wiley & Sons Canada, 2011.

Sylvia Longmire   *Cartel: The Coming Invasion of Mexico's Drug Wars*. New York: Palgrave Macmillan, 2011.

David A. Shirk   *The Drug War in Mexico: Confronting a Shared Threat*. New York: Council on Foreign Relations, 2011.

Peter Watt and Roberto Zepeda   *Drug War Mexico: Politics, Neoliberalism, and Violence in the New Narcoeconomy*. New York: Zed Books, 2012.

Periodicals and Internet Sources

Philip K. Abbott   "The Merida Initiative: A Flawed Counterdrug Policy?," *Small Wars Journal*, January 6, 2011. http://small warsjournal.com.

Julián Aguilar   "In Mexico, a New Approach to Stanching Drug Violence," *New York Times*, December 29, 2012. www.ny times.com.

Fulton T. Armstrong	"End the Drug War," *Foreign Policy*, March 20, 2012. www.foreignpolicy.com.
John Bolton	"The Threat South of the Border: Mexico's Drug War Endangers US Interests. Obama Must Wake Up," *New York Daily News*, October 6, 2010. www.nydailynews.com.
Robert C. Bonner	"The Cartel Crackdown: Winning the Drug War and Rebuilding Mexico in the Process," *Foreign Affairs*, May–June 2012. www.foreignaffairs.com.
William Booth	"Mexico's Crime Wave Has Left About 25,000 Missing, Government Documents Show," *Washington Post*, November 29, 2012. www.washingtonpost.com.
Rory Carroll	"Mexico's Drugs War: In the City of Death," *Guardian*, September 16, 2010. www.guardian.co.uk.
Henry Fernandez	"Death at the Border," *Center for American Progress*, August 31, 2010. www.americanprogress.org.
Ioan Grillo	"Hit Mexico's Cartels with Legalization," *New York Times*, November 1, 2012. www.nytimes.com.

Mark Kleiman "Surgical Strikes in the Drug Wars: Smarter Policies for Both Sides of the Border," *Foreign Affairs*, September–October 2011. www.foreignaffairs .com.

Martin A. Lee "Victory for Pot Means Beginning of the End of Our Crazy Drug War," *Daily Beast*, November 8, 2012. www.thedailybeast.com.

Andres Martinez "Distant Neighbors," *Slate*, April 14, 2009. www.slate.com.

Tim Padgett "Can Mexico's Presidential Hopefuls Stop the Bodies Piling Up?," *Time*, May 15, 2012. www.time.com.

Alfonso Serrano "How Latin America May Lead the World in Decriminalizing Drug Use," *Time*, October 9, 2012. www.time .com.

Michael Weissenstein "Mexico's Cartels Build Own National Radio System," *Salon*, December 26, 2011. www.salon.com.

Index